BC[illegible]OLLED DIET

BY
RAYMOND WARRILLOW

For most people, the Body-Controlled Diet (the BC Diet) is the only way to lose weight and stay slim. It is safe and does not include taking drugs, counting calories, weighing food, eating special food, or joining diet clubs.

ISBN 978-1-909435-80-3

BODY-CONTROLLED DIET

CONTENTS

CHAPTER 1
WHY IS LOSING WEIGHT SO DIFFICULT?

CHAPTER 2
WHY DOES THE WEIGHT THAT IS LOST ON A DIET NEARLY ALWAYS RETURN?

CHAPTER 3
HOW TO DECEIVE THE CLEVER, LITTLE KNOW-ALL.

CHAPTER 4
HOW TO EXERCISE TO INCREASE YOUR METABOLIC RATE AND PREVENT YOUR BASAL METABOLIC RATE FROM FALLING.

CHAPTER 5
HOW TO REDUCE YOUR FOOD INTAKE.

CHAPTER 6
THE TIME IT SHOULD TAKE FOR YOU TO LOSE WEIGHT.

CHAPTER 7
RECOMMENDED FOODS TO SUPPLY ALL OF YOUR NUTRITIONAL NEEDS.

CHAPTER 8
FOOD LISTS.

CHAPTER 9
BODY-CONTROLLED DIET AT A GLANCE.

CHAPTER 10
A WIDER VIEW OF NUTRITION WITH USEFUL TIPS AND INFORMATION.

CHAPTER 11
WHY DOES THE BRAIN EAT THE BODY ON A CRASH DIET?

CHAPTER 12
THE STIMULI THE HYPOTHALAMUS NEEDS TO ACTIVATE THE STARVATION RESPONSE.

CHAPTER 13
HOW MUCH WEIGHT TO LOSE EACH WEEK?

CHAPTER 14
AN EXPLANATION OF MY CLAIM.

CHAPTER 1

WHY IS LOSING WEIGHT SO DIFFICULT?

Why is losing weight and staying slim so difficult when all the weight-reduction diets being sold today are guaranteed to work? The reason is that even though the diets guarantee you will lose weight, you nearly always put the weight back on again, and usually within a few months. It is true to say that trying to lose weight and stay slim is a waste of time and money because you end up looking and weighing exactly the same after your diet as you did before. The ever-growing number of overweight people who buy these guaranteed diets testifies to this sad but true fact. They desperately want to lose weight, but instead of staying slim, their weight yo-yos up and down with each new diet they try, and they are left feeling frustrated, depressed and overweight.

You are probably wondering why dieters regain the weight they lose. You may believe it is because they are weak, greedy or inferior to slim people in some way. You would be wrong. The reason why dieters find it so difficult to lose weight and stay slim is because of a survival mechanism called the starvation response. We are all genetically programmed with many survival mechanisms. They are lifesavers, although there is one we could well do without, and that is the starvation response. If we cannot find enough food to eat and are forced to live off the food stored in our adipose tissue (body fat), the starvation response is activated. The starvation response has one main function, and that is to make sure that the fat taken out of the adipose tissue is returned as soon as food becomes available.

The body regards a weight-reduction diet as a famine and thinks we are starving to death. The starvation response helped our ancestors survive famines when food was scarce. Our ancestors survived by living on the food stored in their bodies as fat. The starvation response makes sure that the fat is returned to the body so it can be used during the next famine. Today, it is very different. We do not have to survive famines, but our bodies are still programmed with the starvation response, so that when we lose weight on a diet, the weight always returns.

It took me many years of research to find a way to avoid the starvation response and the cravings so that we could lose weight and stay slim. All you have to do to lose weight and stay slim is to read this book. I will explain what the cravings are later in the book.

We all possess a starvation response written into our genes. The starvation response makes sure that all the fat is replaced if it is used during a food shortage. The body returns the fat in the same way that it returns blood that is lost from the body. If we give a pint of blood to a hospital, we do not walk around with an empty arm.

We cannot change our genes, so how can we avoid the starvation response? How can we lose weight and stay slim? I will now explain how this can be done.

The hypothalamus in our brain controls the starvation response and reacts to the stimuli it receives.

The only way we can change the genetic instructions regarding the starvation response is by tricking the hypothalamus into believing that the removal of fat from the body is not because of a famine. The hypothalamus receives five stimuli from the body to tell it that it is a famine. If the BC Diet is followed, the hypothalamus will only receive two stimuli. If the hypothalamus only receives two stimuli (when five are required), the starvation response will not be activated. When the starvation response is not activated, any weight lost on a diet will not be returned, and the person will stay slim.

The BC Diet is the only diet that recommends altering the stimuli that the hypothalamus receives.

Many people have experienced the frustration of being a failed dieter and are now thoroughly disillusioned. They have tried to diet, religiously following the maker's instructions for many different kinds of diets, but after all their hard work, they find themselves back where they started: overweight and depressed.

Many struggle for years, sometimes even obtaining their ideal weight, only to find that the fat returns a few months later. A few never give up and resort to trying any new diet, however bizarre, and spend their entire lives dieting. Others eventually accept defeat and buy tent-like clothing to hide their predicament. These unhappy people are forced to change their lifestyle to that of an overweight person.

When an overweight person eventually realises, after trying many diets, that they cannot lose weight and stay slim and that they are always going to be overweight, they resort to telling fibs. This is because they feel guilty. They feel that they have failed. The reason for this feeling of guilt is that all diets are guaranteed to work, so it must be their fault if they have failed to lose weight and stay slim.

Try harder, be determined, and do not give up, friends may say to encourage the overweight person, implying that it is only a matter of willpower to lose weight and stay slim and that all anyone needs to do is to eat less. It is inevitable that when they fail to lose weight and stay slim, they will be regarded as weak and inferior and as misfits in society. They will then have to carry the yolk of failure and bear the brunt of many cruel jokes.

It is painful, depressing, and extremely frustrating to be overweight and to have failed in what is supposed to be a relatively easy task and to be trapped forever in a body that is larger than you want, a body that advertises to the world your problems, your inabilities and your weaknesses. It is even more frustrating when you know that you are not weak or inferior and that you do not lack willpower.

It is all too easy to give up dieting and to take the easy way out and say that you prefer being overweight. Society may regard your choice as a little odd, but at least you will not be regarded as weak-willed and as a failure.

The media has relentlessly reinforced the idea that it is the thin person who is intelligent, successful, sexy, brave, etc., which, of course, implies that overweight people are unintelligent, unsuccessful, unattractive and cowardly. The image of this thin person that bombards us in films, advertising, television, magazines, etc, is so powerful that it can make the overweight person try to be too slim. It can force them to aim at a totally unrealistic weight. This media pressure can even make healthy people who are only a few pounds overweight feel that they should diet and that they are inferior to thin people.

We all accept that being overweight can be unhealthy, but being thin can also be unhealthy, especially when you have a large frame. Many people, especially women, try to lose weight when there is no physical or medical reason to. The media puts pressure on them until they become obsessed with dieting, counting calories, and weighing themselves. Being even a few pounds overweight can be seen by some women as a threat to their sexuality and their womanhood. Some even become ill in their effort to achieve this modern concept of a perfect shape. It is a very sad state indeed.

It is important for you to ignore media trends and fashions and decide for yourself what size you want to be. You need to analyse your preferences, age, and lifestyle, and not follow what is currently fashionable.

If you are considering having weight-loss injections, it is very important to see your doctor first. It does not matter how you lose weight; if you do not follow the BC Diet, you will put all the weight you lose back on again. The clever little know-all will see to that.

Despite the fact that their diets do not work, the dieting industry is booming and making a great deal of money. They focus on the wants of the overweight public, using slogans such as, lose weight fast, quick weight loss, weight loss in days, etc. They know that dieters want to lose weight fast, so they use this knowledge to promote their diets. They offer the dieter what the dieter wants, but ignore their needs. The dieter may want to lose weight fast, but their need is to lose weight and stay slim. The dieter's desire is to be slim for the rest of their life and not just for a few weeks.

People who are overweight are sick of being told that they are greedy or weak and that losing weight and staying slim is just a matter of willpower. They are sick of being told to change their eating habits, to think thin, to eat only when hungry, to eat off a smaller plate, to chew each mouthful thirty times, to not eat between meals, to weigh their food, to count calories; to eat only certain combinations of foods; to go to diet clubs; to exercise; to not eat foods they like; to eat plenty of carrots; etc. etc. The list is almost endless; all well-meaning but useless.

Overweight people have been railroaded into diet clubs, herded into keep-fit classes, exploited, misled and made the objects of derision. They have been treated like naughty little children who secretly gorge themselves on sweets and cakes. They have suffered long enough. It is time for the true facts to be told.

The first and most important true fact is that dieters are not to blame for the failure of modern diets. They are not to blame at all. They are the innocent ones. They have been advised by the manufacturers of modern diets to go against nature and try to change innate biological mechanisms that are impossible to change. It is like asking a man to will his beard to stop growing. It cannot be done.

The blame for the failure of modern diets lies entirely with the diets themselves. They simply do not work. They do not give the dieter what the dieter needs. They can only induce a temporary weight loss. They cannot make overweight people slim. But what about the guarantee that you will lose weight that comes with every diet? Surely, it is illegal to guarantee something that does not work. It is time to expose the diet guarantee for what it really is, in its true colours.

All modern diets guarantee that you will lose weight if you buy their product. This implies that all diets work. The problem is you put all the weight back on again that you lost on the diet, and you end up looking and weighing exactly the same as you did before. This is because the body is genetically programmed to replace any lost weight in the same way that a man's beard is genetically programmed to grow and broken bones are genetically programmed to mend. This fact is not explained to the person who buys the diet. They are left in the dark. They are under the impression that the weight they lose will stay off, but this is not the case.

A legal loophole protects the diet manufacturers, and they are able to guarantee weight loss because there will be a weight loss (albeit a temporary one), and so they are legally protected, but are they morally right to mislead the public? I believe that they are not.

The weight that a dieter loses, which makes the diet guarantee legal, is not just fat. On these fast weight-reduction diets, a dieter will initially lose mostly water and glycogen. Glycogen is an insoluble form of sugar that is stored in the liver and muscles for use in an emergency, such as when running for a bus. It will be lost very quickly, but it will also be replaced very quickly.

The stating of this fact always produces the same unanimous and rehearsed response from manufacturers of modern diets. But you will also lose fat on our diet; look at these before and after pictures. This is where you need to keep your wits about you. This is where the diet manufacturers become very clever and very cunning.

It is true that a dieter will lose fat on any of these modern diets if they remain on them long enough, but they will put the fat that they lose back on again in a very short time. This is not because they are weak or inferior. It is because they are genetically programmed with a survival mechanism they inherited from their ancestors.

Diet manufacturers do not have a diet that will make a fat person slim, and so they offer them a dream, a dream that takes the form of a temporary reduction in weight. This offers the dieter a glimpse of what they would look like if they were slim. But is it fair to the millions of people who spend small fortunes on these diets to spend their entire lives pursuing what is only a dream, a dream that will eventually turn into a nightmare? It is not only unfair, it is scandalous.

People who buy these diets in good faith should be told that they can expect to put all of the weight they lose back on again. They should be told the truth and not deceived into thinking that a guarantee means that they will stay slim.

The diet manufacturers are now desperate. Their diets have been exposed as a waste of time, and their guarantees as not being worth the paper they are written on. They do not want to lose what is, after all, a lucrative industry, so they play their ace card, which they intend to be their winning card. Some people do lose weight on our diet and stay slim, they claim confidently.

This statement, as strange as it may seem, is true. A very small number of people do lose weight on all modern diets and stay slim. The reason why this happens has nothing at all to do with any one particular kind of diet. This remarkable phenomenon occurs to a few people irrespective of what diet they follow. It has been a mystery for many years why some people stay slim, and it has been a scapegoat for diet manufacturers. It has been their winning card. They have been able to claim that some of their dieters have remained slim. Our diets work, they proclaim.

The knowledge that some people remain slim after dieting makes those who have put their weight back on again feel even more guilty and even more convinced that it must be their fault that they have failed.

The answer to this strange phenomenon has nothing at all to do with modern diets. They are still a complete waste of time and money. The reason for the very small success rate is analogous to the fact that if hundreds of people were put into a large maze, a few would invariably find their way out. Not because they knew the way, but by chance.

With modern diets, it is by chance that some dieters stay slim and not by design. It is an accident, a pleasant one, maybe, but still an accident. The dieters who stayed slim are unable to explain what it was that they did that was different to those who put their weight back on again. They may have found their way out of the maze, but they are unable to draw a map for others to follow.

The few who remain slim can very easily begin to see themselves as being superior to the failed dieter. They may have succeeded in losing weight, but they are not superior, and they do not possess any more willpower. Their success has nothing at all to do with any of their personal qualities. It was by chance alone that the weight they lost stayed off. Modern dieting is very chancy. It is a gamble with odds of almost a hundred to one. It is no wonder so many people give up dieting and remain overweight.

About forty years ago, I became aware of this strange phenomenon, and I believed that if some people could lose weight and stay slim, then it should be possible for everyone to lose weight and stay slim. We all belong to the same species of mammal called Homo sapiens, and so should be genetically similar. This means we should all possess the ability to stay slim.

I was determined to discover why the weight lost on a diet sometimes stays off so that I could lose weight and stay slim. I also intended to understand the biological processes involved so that I would be able to explain it to other overweight people, so that they would also be able to lose weight and stay slim.

I intended not only to find my way out of the maze but also to make a map of the way out. It was a task that took me many long years of studying and researching.

During my teens, I found it easy to lose weight, but the weight always returned. Within a few months, I would end up weighing exactly the same as before. I was a keen sportsman, and I found being overweight distasteful and extremely frustrating. Every year, I would embark on a weight-reduction diet, determined that this time I would stay slim. I would lose weight and vow never to let it return, but it did. It always returned.

After many years of trying every conceivable way to stay slim, I began to analyse how I felt when the weight returned. It soon became obvious to me that willpower alone could not prevent the weight returning. There was something else involved. I was determined to find what this something else was.

Within a short time, my research and studying began in earnest. I collected data on other people's efforts to lose weight, as well as on my own, on when they started to diet, how much weight they lost, and when the weight returned. I found from my studies that a person could lose weight and keep it off if the weight had been gained during the previous twelve months. But if the person had been overweight for more than twelve months, the body would regard their new weight as their normal weight and would make sure that it was always returned within a few months.

It is possible to put on a few pounds over Christmas and lose them in the spring. The body does not return this weight. But if you leave it until the following spring before losing weight, the body will by then regard the extra fat as part of your body, and even though it can be lost on a diet, it will always be returned. I would ponder for hours on why the body should react in such a way. I was by now fully aware of the problem, but still without an answer.

For some strange reason, I believed that one day I would find the answer, so I continued to search. I began to study anything and everything that was even remotely connected to losing weight. I felt that knowledge held the answer. I not only studied every aspect of nutrition, but also studied plant, animal, and human biology. I became a physiologist and delved into microbiology, chemistry, physiology, ecology, food chains and food production. I left no stone unturned.

The studying was intensive and far-reaching, but I was not even warm. I still did not have a clue. It was very frustrating. It was only when my studies of animal physiology led via genetics to evolution and how mankind used to live thousands of years ago that the pieces began to slowly fall into place.

If we use a jigsaw to represent the complete picture of weight-reduction dieting (each separate jigsaw piece analogous to one piece of knowledge), the picture would contain many thousands of pieces and would cover many different subjects.

To obtain a clear picture of all the problems involved in losing weight so that an answer could be found as to why the weight returns, I needed to study all of the knowledge contained on all of the different jigsaw pieces. A few pieces will not give an overall picture. It was a very laborious and time-consuming task.

Many experts today specialise due to the vast amount of knowledge needed to understand any one subject, and so they would only have the knowledge contained on a few pieces of such a large jigsaw. They would not see the whole picture. If, for instance, they studied biology, they would probably concentrate or major on one small part of the subject, such as genetics, microbiology, or nutrition. Even those studying nutrition would major in areas that would lead to a career, such as dietetics or the food manufacturing industry. They may even specialise in diets for athletes, bodybuilders, pregnant women, or children, but not in weight-reduction dieting. Helping people to lose weight has not been seen as a worthwhile area of study.

The reason why experts have been reluctant to specialise in weight reduction dieting is because they believe the problem is self-inflicted. They believe overweight people to be either greedy or lacking willpower. One only needs to eat less to lose weight, they say. They do not see the problem as needing professional attention.

Obesity and anorexia are diseases that are linked closely to psychological disorders and should, of course, be treated by a medically trained doctor, but being one, two, or three stone overweight is not classed as a disease and is more often regarded by the medical profession as unimportant, and due only to overeating.

In my studies, I found weight-reduction dieting to be a very complicated subject and not as straightforward as it may seem at first. To major in weight-reduction dieting, there is a need for knowledge not only of biology and nutrition but also of physiology, psychology, diseases and evolution. The picture can only be seen clearly if all the jigsaw pieces are used.

As time went by, I added many new jigsaw pieces until, eventually, a picture began to emerge. It took many years to formulate my theory (my hypothesis), but when I did, I was totally convinced that I had found the answer. I believed that I had at last discovered a way to lose weight and stay slim. I believed that when I lost weight this time, it would stay off. I was eager to become the guinea pig for my new diet.

Normally, any weight I lose on a diet would slowly return over about two to three months, but this time it was different. After losing weight, I remained slim. I did not experience the cravings, and I did not put the weight back on. Even to this day, the weight has never returned. I had finally discovered a way to lose weight and stay slim. I had found a way to get out of the maze.

It was an exhilarating feeling to be in control of my body and to be able to decide how much fat I carried around with me. People who have a weight problem will understand the joy that I felt. To cut a long story short, I began what turned out to be a five-year special study of dieting and nutrition to evaluate and test my hypothesis and to make sure that my map of how to get out of the maze was accurate as well as easy for others to follow.

CHAPTER 2

WHY DOES THE WEIGHT THAT IS LOST ON A DIET NEARLY ALWAYS RETURN?

To find your way out of the maze so that you can lose weight and stay slim, all you need to do is read this book and follow the diet. If you are not interested in the details of how to get out of the maze and just want to lose weight, then go to Chapter 9, The BC Diet at a Glance. If you do want to understand all the details involved, then read on. The subject is extremely complicated, but I will do my best to make it as interesting and easy to understand as possible.

The human body is infinitely complicated and can perform biological miracles. It can, with the aid of what we call enzymes, do things that scientists cannot do in the laboratory, at least not without extremely high temperatures or very strong acids. The body is so complicated that the combined efforts of all the twenty-first-century boffins have as yet been unable to unravel many of its secrets.

One of the many complex abilities the body has is balancing its internal environment, a process called homeostasis. For the body to work properly, it must maintain a constant level of water, pH, temperature, hormones, blood sugar, and other essential processes. If these levels fluctuate, we could become ill, and if they stray too far from the optimum level, we could die. They are processes we take for granted in our everyday lives.

The body, as we all know, can maintain a constant internal temperature despite fluctuations in the external environment. It is so clever at maintaining a constant level that doctors can ascertain whether someone is ill simply by taking their temperature. An individual's state of health, as well as their life, depends on a correct homeostatic balance. The body needs a constant core temperature so that its many enzymes can function at their best.

Homeostatic levels are controlled by a part of the forebrain called the hypothalamus. The hypothalamus regulates many physiological states, such as temperature, thirst, hunger, water excretion, breathing, heart rate, blood pressure and even sleep patterns. If we were to cut open the hypothalamus and examine it, we would find a mass of flesh and blood about the size of a thumb. It would not give us any clues as to how it works. It is extremely difficult to understand how it manages to cope with the many highly complex regulatory mechanisms required to balance the body's homeostatic levels.

Research and study in this area may be interesting to the boffins but not to the average person, so I do not intend to even try to explain how these mechanisms work. For the purpose of this book, it is easier and more interesting to think of the hypothalamus as a control room that is supervised by a little man. A little man who has many instruments and computers to help him control and regulate the body's many homeostatic levels. For instance, to tell him the body's current temperature and the temperature it should be. He is very good at his job and very keen, which is why the body temperature is always 98.6 degrees Fahrenheit (37 degrees Celsius). To be scientifically correct, each healthy individual can have a slightly different set level of temperature, such as 98.5 or 98.7 degrees Fahrenheit.

If the body gets too cold, the little man in control moves the blood away from the skin, induces shivering and persuades the individual to put on more clothes or to seek a warmer place to sit. If, on the other hand, the body gets too hot, the little man moves the blood towards the skin, induces sweating and persuades the individual to take off some clothes or to seek a cooler place to sit.

The little man has many hundreds of different jobs to do and is a very clever little man indeed. His control room is chock-a-block with instruments, such as dials, charts and computers, which he is an expert at using. He has, over many thousands of years of evolution, developed these skills to a high level of perfection and, in doing so, has helped the human race survive.

This clever little man also knows how much fat you have stored in your adipose tissue, which he can also regulate. If it is removed either by famine or by dieting, he will make sure that it is replaced. He is, in fact, to blame for the failure of modern diets. It is his fault that overweight people today find it so difficult to lose weight and stay slim. It is for this reason that I refer to him as the clever, little know-all.

The clever, little know-all has a thermostat to monitor your temperature levels and a fatostat to monitor your fat stores. The thermostat is set at 98.6 degrees

Fahrenheit, but your fatostat is set at your personal fat level and varies from person to person.

The clever little know-all is well prepared and knows just what to do in the event of any emergency. But how is he so well prepared, and how does he know what to do? Who has told him, for instance, that the human body temperature should be 98.6 degrees Fahrenheit?

We all possess a hypothalamus, as well as our own personal clever, little know-all who looks after our body's needs. The strange thing is, all of the clever, little know-alls seem to possess the same degree of knowledge as if they had all graduated from the same university. To understand how they have acquired this knowledge, we need to explore the world of genetics. The mere mention of genetics can seem frightening, but if you have patience, I promise to make genes as interesting and as easy to understand as the hypothalamus and the clever, little know-all.

Genes are small sections of chromosomes that contain the plan of a human being. They possess the details of how a human being should be built, how it should look, and how it should function. In fact, everything about a human being, even the length of the eyelashes, is contained in the genes. Genes are similar to the architectural plans of a building.

All animals and plants are made of cells in the same way that a building is made of bricks. Inside each cell, there is a nucleus, which contains the chromosomes. In human cells, there are forty-six chromosomes. Genes are small sections of these chromosomes. It is remarkable how all the details of a human being that would fill many volumes of an encyclopedia are reduced to a size that is invisible to the naked eye.

There are twenty-three pairs of chromosomes in each cell of a human being. We inherit half, that is, twenty-three chromosomes, from our father and the other twenty-three chromosomes from our mother. Each half of the twenty-three pairs of chromosomes that make up the full complement of forty-six contains a complete plan of a human being. This means that we all inherit two plans of two different individuals.

I have just realised that it is almost impossible to make genetics interesting as well as easy to understand. If it is getting too much for you and you are feeling confused, give it a miss and move on to the paragraph beginning, 'Most people already know quite a lot about genetics.'

There are twenty-three chromosomes in the male sperm and twenty-three chromosomes in the female egg. When they fuse together to form the fertilised egg that will eventually grow into a child, it will contain two plans for a human being. That is forty-six chromosomes, or more accurately, twenty-three pairs.

If the chromosomes containing the two plans did not mix when forming gametes, it would mean that, from any one couple, all the sons would be identical, as would all the daughters. Fortunately, the two plans are mixed by processes called cross-over and independent assortment. It is almost as efficient as putting all the different genes into a box and shaking them up.

After mixing the genes, there are still two separate plans in the form of twenty-three pairs of chromosomes, forty-six in total. In other words, there will be two plans for the length of the eyelashes and two plans for the colour of the eyes, etc. The genes are duplicated. There is one exception. A female has two 'X' chromosomes

(XX), but a male has an 'X' and a 'Y' (XY). These chromosomes determine a person's sex, but let us not get too sidetracked.

Even though it sounds confusing to us, it is not confusing to the body. The body simply separates the genes into two groups, dominant and recessive, and only uses the dominant genes in the plan of the new individual. This means that if one parent passes on the gene for blue eyes and the other parent passes on the gene for brown eyes, the child will receive both genes but will only use one. The child will possess the gene for blue eyes as well as the gene for brown eyes, but it will have brown eyes. This is because the gene for brown eyes is dominant to the gene for blue eyes. The child will still possess the gene for blue eyes, but it will be masked by the gene for brown eyes. The child, when it grows up, will be able to pass on the blue as well as the brown gene for eye colour to his or her children, even though it has brown eyes. Although every individual receives two plans from their parents, only one plan is used: the dominant one.

In every cell of our body, there are forty-six chromosomes (two complete plans), but in sperm and egg cells, the numbers are halved. They contain only one plan, that is, twenty-three chromosomes. This is to enable the twenty-three sperm chromosomes to fuse with the twenty-three egg chromosomes to form a child with a complete set of forty-six chromosomes (two complete plans).

The two plans that the father has can be mixed up with the two plans of the mother in the formation of a new individual. Any combination of the four plans that the parents possess can be used. This is the reason why all children are different. Even if one couple has twenty sons, they will all be different. It is a remarkable process that makes every single human being who has ever lived unique.

If you feel confused about what genes are, then forget all about them. The explanation I have just given is for those who have an inquiring mind. The important thing to remember is that we received our genes from our parents, who received their genes from their parents, and so on. We are all, in this way, connected to our ancestors, even those who lived hundreds of thousands of years ago. We grow according to a plan that, except for a few very minor modifications, is very old indeed.

Most people already know quite a lot about genetics. You know, for instance, that a dog will only give birth to a dog, and a cat will only give birth to a cat. This is because they grow according to the plan on the chromosomes that contain the genes. How often have we heard someone say that a baby has got its father's ears or its mother's eyes? Everyone knows that children always resemble their true parents and grandparents. This is because the genes that contain the complete plan for a human being are passed on from generation to generation.

We all possess a hypothalamus, as well as a clever, little know-all. They are part of everyone's plan. We have also inherited homeostatic levels, such as the temperature level of 98.6 degrees Fahrenheit. We cannot alter these levels because they are in our genes. We are all genetically programmed in a very similar way because we all belong to the same species, called Homo sapiens. We grow to a pre-determined height and size, environment permitting, and we have a pre-determined hair and skin colour. We have no choice but to follow the genetic instructions we inherit from our ancestors. Even many of our conscious thoughts and actions are influenced by our genes.

One of the genetic programs we all possess is the clotting of blood. When we cut ourselves, our blood coagulates; otherwise, we would bleed to death. It is a process most of us take for granted, but it still helps us survive in the same way it helped our ancestors. It is an inherited survival mechanism. We have no control over these inherited, innate biological mechanisms. They occur automatically.

Another genetically inherited program we possess, which was also a survival mechanism for our ancestors, is the return of fat that is lost from the body's adipose tissue. This is also a process that is beyond our control. It is a genetic program and is part of the starvation response.

We can understand how the clotting of blood helped our ancestors and how it was, and still is, a survival mechanism, but how can returning the fat that is lost by the body be a survival mechanism, and how did it help our ancestors to survive? To answer these questions, we need to know a little about evolution.

Evolution is a theory that explains how organisms, such as plants and animals, change and adapt to their surroundings over a long period of time. The better-adapted organisms survive and pass on their genes, whereas the less well-adapted die and so do not pass on their genes. Future generations will always possess the genes from the most successful organisms.

For instance, if an antelope on the African plains did not run fast, it would be eaten by lions. It is the fast-running antelope that survives, grows up, mates, and passes on its genes. The same is true for a lion. If a lion does not learn to hunt, it will die when it leaves its mother. It is the lion that is a good hunter that survives, grows up, mates, and passes on its genes. This process is called natural selection, and all animals, including humans, have been and still are subject to its pressures.

If we possess the inherited ability to replace fat lost on a diet, it must have been beneficial to our ancestors. It must have helped them to survive in some way. If we want to understand why we have inherited this genetic program, we must mentally travel back in time and visit our distant ancestors.

Imagine, if you can, what it must have been like to live in Europe fifty thousand years ago. It would have been a very different world. We would look the same physically and would recognise the different animals and trees, which would also look the same, but our way of life would be completely different. We would have no houses to live in, no books to read and no television to watch. We would be dressed in animal furs and live in caves. It is difficult to imagine that our ancestors lived like this, but they did. They had, by this time, acquired the ability to use fire, not only as a means to keep warm and to cook their food but also as a weapon to ward off attacks by wild animals such as sabre-toothed tigers and mammoths. They had also learned how to use hand axes (sharp stones) as tools, but other than that, they were very primitive and lived almost as wild animals do today.

Imagine that there were two separate tribes living in Europe at this time, with only one possessing the genetic ability to replace the fat lost from the body.

Both tribes settled down in their caves for the winter, knowing there would be very little food until the spring. Instead of a normal winter, it turned out to be an extremely severe one, and neither tribe had any food. They manage to survive, as animals do, by living off the fat stored in their adipose tissue. In the spring, they returned to their normal way of life. There was now plenty to eat.

During the summer, one of the tribes genetically replaced the fat used during the winter by eating a little extra food. The other tribe, which did not have the same genetic programming, did not eat extra food and so did not replace the fat. The following winter was also extremely severe, and once again, there was no food. One tribe was able to live off the fat that they had genetically replaced and so survived the winter, but the other tribe, which had not replaced the fat in their adipose tissue, starved to death.

The tribe that genetically replaced the lost fat survived to have children and pass on their genes to future generations. We are those future generations, and it is their genes that we possess today. We do not possess any of the genes from the people of the other tribe because they became extinct. They died, and so did their genes.

Humans have adapted to this planet, to its atmosphere, to its food and to its seasons. Each cell in our body needs a continual supply of oxygen, but we can breathe continuously because oxygen in the air is always available. We do not have to carry a large bag of oxygen around with us.

Our cells also need a continual supply of food, but food is not always available, so humans and animals need to be able to store food when it is plentiful for use at times when it is scarce, such as during the winter. Storing food as fat around the body provided the answer to this problem. Body fat is now regarded by our body as essential, which is why it is always replaced.

The clever, little know-all that we all possess is unable to see out of his little house (the hypothalamus), and so does not realise that we are now intellectuals and live in a modern world with plenty to eat. He still thinks that during the winter, we live in caves, and if we decide to lose weight, he thinks that we are starving to death and trying to survive on the odd nut and berry. He thinks that by returning the weight we lose, he is helping us to survive in the same way that he helped our ancestors.

Our ancestors were always at the mercy of the elements and had to survive long periods of time without food. They needed the clever little know-all's survival mechanism (the starvation response) to survive, but modern man, with his centrally heated houses and all the food he can eat, does not need this particular mechanism. He does not need it, and he does not want it, but he is stuck with it.

Returning fat that is lost from the body may, in some parts of the third world, still help people to survive, especially if they have to endure long periods of time without food, but in our modern world, where there is plenty of food to eat during the winter, this particular survival mechanism is not needed. It is a nuisance and prevents us from losing weight and staying slim. Returning fat to our adipose tissue is a vestigial remnant from our past that we could well do without.

It is difficult to see ourselves as anything other than twenty-first-century intellectuals. It is difficult to detach our minds and see our bodies for what they are. If we could, we would find that, apart from the mind, we are animals. We are a species of mammal called Homo sapiens and closely related to the apes.

If we were to cut open the body of a chimpanzee and compare it to the inside of a human being, we would find very little difference. You may expect the inside of the chimpanzee to be completely different to the inside of a human being, but this is not the case. They would look almost the same. There would only be very small differences, such as in the length of some bones.

Some people get upset if we compare ourselves to animals, especially to apes. They think that they are above the animals, which, of course, they are, but only because they have a mind; physically, there is very little difference between humans and apes. We are classed as apes.

Let me explain. When we look at a chimpanzee, we can see a physical difference from a human being. A chimpanzee has long body hair, a different face, longer fingers and toes, etc. This is because it is a different species of Hominoidea. If we compare a gorilla to a chimpanzee, we will also see a physical difference. This is because a gorilla is also a different species from a chimpanzee.

In all the species of Hominoidea, there are differences, but there are also similarities. They all possess lips, nostrils, ears, genitals, hair, fingers, not a paw, nails not claws, toes, an Adam's apple, a kneecap, eyelashes, and even a belly button. They all breastfeed their young, who are born vulnerable and need to be carried about and kept warm. They are all born with walking, sucking and grasping reflexes. They live in family groups, display facial expressions and possess the ability to use tools. Even though humans are called the naked ape, they still have body hair (some more than others) just like all Hominoids. Even women, who sometimes feel the need to remove some of this hair by shaving parts of their anatomy, still have this genetic link with their past.

It is not difficult to see that we were once related to other Hominoids, even if the species did separate a few million years ago. We may have different blood groups and proteins to other Hominoids, such as the chimpanzee, but races of human beings also have different blood groups and proteins, hence the need for tissue matching when transplanting organs from one human being to another.

There is also a difference in the outward appearance of the human species. An Australian aborigine, for instance, is very different to an African pygmy, who is, in turn, very different to a white person. This does not mean that they are not all humans; they are. They are all Homo sapiens and related to each other. They have become different races of human beings by being separated for thousands of years. The different species of Hominoidea, such as gibbons, chimpanzees, orangutans, gorillas and humans, have become different species by being separated for a much longer time and so show a greater difference. They are now unable to breed together.

Humans are a separate species that separated from the other Hominoids millions of years ago. The morphology (shape) of all Hominoids may be similar, but the possession of a mind has made the human species very, very different. We now have the ability to do remarkable things, such as plan for the future and read and write. We even have the ability to destroy all life on our planet. We are an exceptional species, but only because of the mind.

Physically, we are now inferior to most animals in terms of strength and speed. We also have inferior senses, such as sight, hearing and smell. Without the mind, we would be unable to compete with other animals and would not survive for very long. We would, in a very short time, become extinct if it were not for the mind.

If, for instance, intelligent beings from outer space visited our planet, they would see all the life forms on this planet objectively and unemotionally. They would see the similarities between the different species of Hominoids and classify humans as part of this group. They would not classify humans in a group with any other animals because we do not resemble them. We only resemble the apes. The birds would also be seen as a distinct group due to the possession of feathers and wings.

These intelligent beings from outer space would see that one group of apes ruled the world and was more intelligent than any other group of animals. If, for instance, it had been a species of bird, an ostrich, that possessed the mind and ruled the world, living in houses and wearing clothes, the visitors from outer space would still regard the ostrich as a bird, even if the ostrich insisted that it was different. I am larger than other birds, it may insist. I lay larger eggs, I don't fly, and I have large, strong legs. The ostrich would still physically be classed as a bird, even though it possessed a mind and classed itself as different.

We may insist that we are not related to other animals and are different, but in reality, we are Hominoids. Our taxonomic classification is that we belong to the Kingdom called Metazoa; the Phylum called Chordata; the Subphylum called Craniata (vertebrates); the Class called Mammals; the Infraclass called Eutheria (placental mammals); the Order called Primates; the Suborder called Anthropoidea; the Superfamily called Hominoidea; the family called Hominidae; the Genus called Homo, and the Species called Sapiens. We cannot alter our phylogeny or our taxonomic classification any more than an ostrich can.

We need to accept that we are mammals if we are to understand what is best for our bodies. We like to pretend, due to our intellectual prowess, that we are completely different to animals, but we are not.

Many women today do not breastfeed their babies, but like all mammals, they still have mammary glands and the hormones that regulate them, producing milk when required. We do not possess ears that move like a dog's ears and that hone in on sound, but we still have ear muscles as vestigial remnants from the time in our past when we did move our ears. We may prefer not to eat meat, but we still have canine teeth from when we did.

We are intellectually different from all other life on Earth, but physically, we are mammals. We still need to eat and drink, and even though we do not like to talk about it, to defecate and urinate. We need to sleep, to have sex, etc. We function physically as mammals and can never escape from our past.

When a woman gets pregnant, she sometimes gets a craving to eat unnatural foods (pica) such as coal or coke. She is following the remnants of genetic instructions that she has inherited from her distant ancestors. These cravings must have been beneficial to her ancestors in some way. Perhaps eating inorganic substances, such as chalk, replaced some of the minerals, such as calcium, that were being taken out of her body and given to the growing baby. It is another example of how our past can still play a part in our lives, even in the twenty-first century. Pica has also been observed in many animals, as well as in children who are deficient in zinc.

You may find it difficult to believe, but not only are all the animals on earth related to each other, but plants are also included in our very large family of life. The earth is filled with every kind of organism that could be imagined, from trees to bacteria and from whales to butterflies. They are all very different to look at, but at a cellular level, they are very similar. The cells of all living creatures on earth, plants, and animals possess an organelle called a mitochondrion. A mitochondrion is very similar to a power station and provides the cell with all the energy it needs for growth and movement by converting ADP to ATP. Even minute lymphocytes (white blood cells) that float around in our blood contain mitochondria.

At a cellular level, there is a universal similarity between all living organisms. For instance, all plants and animals are made of cells that contain a nucleus, a nucleolus, a nuclear envelope, nuclear pores, DNA, RNA, chromatin, ribosomes, rough and smooth endoplasmic reticulum, mitochondria, vacuoles, pinocytotic vesicles, lysosomes, cytoplasm, Golgi vesicles, and a Golgi complex. These similarities are proof that all life on this planet is related and has evolved from the same ancestors that lived about three thousand six hundred million years ago. Some evolved over millions of years into single-celled plants and then into trees; others into single-celled animals and then into multicellular animals and humans. We all possess the same building blocks, showing that we have the same origins. I am not saying that we are plants or apes, but that we are more closely related to apes than to plants in the earth's family of life.

If we examine the cells of an ape, such as a chimpanzee, under an electron microscope and compare them to human cells, they would look the same. There would be very little difference. We are morphologically as well as microscopically very similar. The only real difference is that we possess a mind.

The link tying all the organisms on this planet together into one family is an intangible energy that we call life. It makes us all part of one family. The mind, as well as this life force, transcends all human knowledge and experience. It is as yet beyond our understanding.

I am not advocating for one moment that we should act like animals or that there is not a god. All I am saying is that human beings have physically evolved on this planet in the same way that other creatures have and have adapted to its atmosphere, its climate of wind, rain, humidity and temperature; to its variable terrain, its changing seasons; its supply of food and water, as well as, ecologically, to all other living organisms. Our bodies are the result of millions of years of evolution and adaptation.

We are not the only mammals to have acquired the ability to store a reserve of fuel (fat) in their adipose tissue. It is a process used by many animals to help them survive long periods without food, such as during long, foodless winters. For example, the grizzly bear that sleeps through the cold part of the winter also survives by living off the fat that is stored in its adipose tissue. It puts on about thirty kilograms of fat before its hibernation. At the end of the winter, the bear does not think, 'I will have to eat extra food; otherwise, I will not survive the next winter.' The bear does not have to do anything; its body does it for it. The bear is genetically programmed to eat extra food so that the fat in its adipose tissue is replaced each time it is used. By possessing this genetically inherited mechanism, the bear is able to survive winter after winter after winter.

There are many examples of how fat is genetically controlled and used by animals. A mouse doubles its weight before hibernation. A red deer whose rut lasts for two months does not eat at all during the rut and lives off the fat that is stored in its adipose tissue. A polar bear gives birth in its den of snow and feeds its young for many weeks without feeding.

If we see ourselves as we really are, in flesh-and-blood terms, we will be able to decide what is best for our bodies, such as what food to eat and what exercise to do. Ignoring that we are mammals will only confuse the issue and make finding answers to our nutritional and weight problems more difficult.

We are an integral and intrinsic part of the Earth and the life on it, and not some alien life form visiting from another galaxy. The atoms in our bodies that we use have been used many times before by other humans. They have also been used by animals, plants and even dinosaurs. We drink water that contains molecules that have been drunk many times before. Your faith and beliefs are personal to you and have nothing at all to do with me or anyone else, but your body is the physical part of your entity and, as such, is a part of the earth. It has physical needs, and one of those needs is food that it has adapted to over a very long period of time.

Now that you have a greater understanding of why your bodies are built the way they are, especially why you have fat, let's return to the clever, little know-all who is determined to keep what fat you have where it is. His determination is admirable, although very frustrating.

The clever, little know-all regulates your body's fat deposits in the same way he regulates your temperature. If you are too hot, he makes physical changes in your body, such as making you sweat, but he also changes how you think. He makes you desire to be cooler. He makes you feel uncomfortable so that you will take off some clothes or seek a cooler place to sit. If you ignore him, he will make your life a misery. He intends to get his own way and will not rest until he has reduced your temperature. He is a very determined little fellow.

If you lose weight and reduce the amount of fat that is in your adipose tissue, the clever, little know-all will want to return all the fat that you have lost and will make physical changes in your body, such as lowering your metabolic rate (MR) and your basal metabolic rate (BMR). He will also change the way you think by making you hungrier than normal, so that you will eat more than your body needs. This particular kind of hunger is different to normal hunger, which is why I refer to it as psychological cravings.

Hunger and satiety are very complicated processes. They are normally in line with your metabolism, so you eat just enough food to meet your body's needs. This means you eat just enough calories to fuel the body. If you eat too little, you will die, and if you eat too much, you will become overweight.

As children, we are very energetic and use up a lot of energy. In other words, we burn a lot of calories by running about and growing. When we stop growing and running about, our metabolism slows down, and so we reduce our food intake accordingly. We will now only eat as much food as our particular lifestyle demands. The process that adapts our food intake to our energy needs, that is, the calorie intake to the calories used, is not controlled by us. We play no part in it. It is controlled by the clever, little know-all.

Over thousands of years, the human body has evolved extremely complex mechanisms to deal with nutrient deficiencies, but it has never evolved a mechanism to cope with excess food. The body does not regard eating too much food as a problem, so the clever, little know-all is happy to store it away as fat. This means you will get fatter and fatter if you eat in excess to your body's needs.

It is only very recently that mankind has been able to eat too much. Until about a hundred years ago, humans had a diet that was almost impossible to get fat on. It was low in sugar and fat and high in fibre. Today, we have a diet high in sugar and fat and much lower in fibre. The only sugar our ancestors had was naturally occurring in fruit and vegetables or as honey. Even fat was less abundant. The meat that was available to them was the lean meat from wild animals and not the fatty meat from modern domestic animals that are bred to be fat. Our distant ancestors would have been hunter-gatherers and would have been slim. They would not have been overweight.

The recent change in our diet has resulted in obesity and weight problems, and because our lifestyle is so very different (we spend most of our time sitting down), we are also unfit, as well as overweight. Our bodies have not been programmed for a leisurely life, and function at their best with plenty of exercise. They have also not been programmed for a diet that is high in sugar and fat and low in fibre. It is no wonder that there are so many people suffering from heart disease, diabetes, high blood pressure, strokes, gallbladder and large bowel diseases, piles, joint problems, breathlessness, varicose veins, and psychological problems due to excess weight.

What do you think would happen if you exchanged the diet of a giant panda that eats mostly bamboo shoots with the diet of a koala bear that eats mostly eucalyptus leaves? The answer is they would both die. If the diet of any animal, including humans, is changed drastically, it will cause illness and even death. Humans have changed their diet drastically and are now suffering from the consequences.

The clever, little know-all adjusts our food intake in line with our needs. He is usually very good at this. He makes us hungry when we need food, and so we eat. He then makes us feel satisfied when we have eaten enough, and so we stop eating. It sounds very simple, but do not be deceived. This process involves the vagus nerve, stomach receptors, the nervous system, hormones, blood sugar levels, the hypothalamus, the brain, and almost the entire body. It is so complicated that science does not understand exactly how it works. I told you what a clever, little fellow the clever, little know-all is.

If you eat more than you need, especially foods such as chocolate, sweets and cakes (foods that our ancestors did not eat), the clever, little know-all will store the extra calories away in the body's larder as fat. He will continue storing the extra food away because our bodies have no way of telling him that the larder is full. You will get fatter, and fatter, and fatter.

There is also a genetic factor that plays a part in why a person puts on weight. Some people are genetically programmed to absorb all the food they eat, and so will find it very easy to put on weight. Their poo will contain very little food. Other people absorb only what they need from their food and remain slim. Their poo will contain a large amount of food. We all know people who eat huge amounts of cakes, sweets and chocolates and remain slim. What is aggravating is when these people accuse the rest of us of being greedy. The cheeky little devils.

If you are one of the unfortunate individuals who retain every calorie you eat, and you decide to try one of the many modern diets on sale today, the clever, little know-all will think that you are suffering from a famine and will react accordingly. He is an expert at reacting to a famine and knows exactly what to do. He has all the information he needs contained in the genes that you inherited from your ancestors.

The first thing the clever, little know-all does is make you ravenously hungry. This is to make sure that if there is any food available, you will eat it, but if you are determined to lose weight, you will refuse to eat extra food. After a few days, the clever, little know-all reduces these hunger pangs by lowering the hunger level that is in his little control room. He now knows that it is a famine. You are still hungry but not ravenously hungry. It would be pointless making you ravenously hungry if it was a famine because there would be no food available for you to eat. It may be a diet to you, but it is a famine to the clever, little know-all.

To conserve fuel, the clever, little know-all lowers your MR and BMR in the same way that you would switch off a few lights to reduce your electricity bill. He thinks that your life depends on his efforts to conserve energy. In the first few days of a low-calorie diet, you will use glucose, glycogen and fat as fuel. After a few more days, you will also begin to use protein (lean tissue) as fuel. You may be surprised to learn that the body uses protein from muscles as well as fat from the adipose tissue when you go on a low-calorie diet. I will explain more about this process later in the book.

Eventually, you decide that you have lost sufficient weight and begin to eat normally again. The extra food that is now coming into your body tells the clever, little know-all that the famine is over and that there is now plenty of food to eat. This stage in your diet would have coincided with the arrival of spring for our distant ancestors, when food became plentiful. The clever, little know-all now raises your hunger and satiety levels so that you will eat just a little more than you would normally eat to maintain your life processes. This is to make sure that you slowly replace all the fat you have lost. The clever little know-all remembers exactly how much fat you have lost in the same way that he remembers what temperature you should be if you become too hot or too cold.

If you try to resist eating extra food, you will find yourself under extreme pressure, and you will begin to crave food full of sugar and fat. The clever little know-all is determined to make you eat more and will keep raising your hunger level until you are ravenously hungry. Even after finishing a normal-sized meal, you will feel as if you are starving to death. He slowly destroys your willpower in a war of attrition. He is a very determined little fellow.

These cravings you feel for foods full of sugar and fat are not normal hunger pangs. They are powerful psychological cravings and similar to the cravings that some pregnant women have for chalk or coal. They have nothing to do with normal hunger pangs.

If you do not eat extra food, these cravings become more intense, and you will feel ill if you try to resist them. The longer you resist, the worse you feel. The only relief you get is when you eat an extra sandwich, some extra potatoes, or a chocolate bar. These cravings are so strong that nearly everyone succumbs to them; I always did. They are difficult to explain to someone who has never been on a diet. You will need to experience them for yourself to understand just how powerful they are.

The clever, little know-all is desperate to return all the weight that you have lost because he knows that in a few months, there will be another famine (the arrival of the next foodless winter), and if you do not replace all the fat and lean tissue that you have lost, you will starve to death. He does not realise that it is not a famine and that you have deliberately lost weight on a weight-reduction diet.

If the clever, little know-all is so powerful and impossible to resist, how are we going to prevent him from returning all the weight that we lose on a diet? How are we going to stay slim? We cannot change our genetic inheritance (our genes) any more than we can change our sex. So how are we going to convince the clever, little know-all that it is not a famine? The answer is, we trick him. We mislead him into thinking that everything is normal and that we are not starving to death. He will then not return the weight that we lose on a diet. (It's getting very exciting, isn't it?)

In reality, the hypothalamus reacts to the stimuli it receives. It does not think. If it receives a specific stimulus, it reacts in a specific way. The BC Diet changes the stimuli the hypothalamus receives, so it does not react by promoting processes that return the fat lost on a diet. The workings of the hypothalamus can be a little confusing, and it is far better to think of it in terms of a control room and a clever, little know-all than processes such as esterification, gluconeogenesis, glycogenolysis, glycolysis, glycogenesis, lipolysis, etc, etc.

For those with an inquiring mind, I will give a brief explanation as to what happens when we lose weight. The timing mechanisms that control when and how much we eat are situated in our hypothalamus in an area called the suprachiasmatic nucleus. There are two nuclei in the anterior part of the hypothalamus, which contain the main biological clocks that control the body's other clocks and circadian, circalunar and circannual rhythms. We are all affected by these endogenous rhythms. A woman's period, for instance, is timed by a twenty-eight-day circalunar rhythm, as is her pregnancy, which is nine lunar months long. A lunar month is approximately twenty-nine days long.

The fat in our adipose tissue is also controlled by biological clocks. If fat is removed from the adipose tissue, the clock ticks away, and if the fat is not returned, the clever, little know-all gets to work. He keeps moving the set point in your hypothalamus (making you hungrier and hungrier) until you eat a little extra food at each mealtime.

To show you just how the hypothalamus knows how much fat is stored in the body, we need to examine the lifestyle of a small bird. This bird, which also has its own clever, little know-all, leaves the British shores in spring and migrates to Ellesmere Island, northwest of Greenland. The bird (a knot) makes the journey in two stages. For the first stage of its migration, it increases its body weight by 30%. It then uses this fat to fuel its journey to Iceland. It then feeds in Iceland and increases its body weight by 40% to fuel its journey to northern Greenland.

The clever, little know-all of the bird allows the bird to begin its migration only when the required 30% of fat is stored in the bird's adipose tissue. The bird is then instructed to begin its journey. When the bird reaches Iceland, the clever, little know-all causes the bird to eat extra food until its body weight has increased by 40%.

It then tells the bird to begin the second part of its migration.

This simple example shows how the hypothalamus knows exactly how much fat is stored in the body and how it can adjust that amount according to genetic instructions. We also have genetic instructions controlling our stores of fat. They are different instructions to those given to a bird, but they are there, and control how we use fat, when we use it, and when and if it is returned.

Biological clocks time and control many aspects of our everyday life. Circadian rhythms (twenty-four-hour rhythms) are the reason why we suffer from jet lag when we travel across time zones to another country. The effects of jet lag can last several days until our endogenous (internal) clocks re-entrain to the new day and night times. Light penetrates into the brain and can be detected by the hypothalamus, so the clever, little know-all knows when it is day or night. These light and dark periods act as zeitgebers (timekeepers) for our endogenous clocks.

Circadian rhythms also control our sleeping patterns, which are genetically programmed and differ from animal to animal. A shrew appears never to sleep, while a sloth sleeps for up to twenty out of every twenty-four hours.

If we deliberately disobey instructions from our body, such as the genetic instructions to sleep, we will find that our body will eventually get its way. After a few days of increasing tiredness, we will fall asleep. The same is true about the biological clocks that control the timing of when the fat that is lost on a diet should be returned. If we refuse to eat extra food to replace the fat, the clever, little know-all will make us feel ill. We will feel as if we are starving to death. Some people feel faint or suffer from depression or anxiety. Eventually, the clever, little know-all will get his way, and we will eat the extra food that is needed to replace the fat that we lost on our diet.

We will not be able to resist eating the extra food any more than we can resist sleep. We can put up a fight, but we will lose eventually. The cravings are too powerful to resist. The clever, little know-all intends to win and usually does. By understanding physiology (how everything works in conjunction with everything else), we can do remarkable things. We can deceive our clever, little know-all by altering the information he receives. Our biological clocks will then be altered, and the weight that we lose on a diet will not be returned.

CHAPTER 3

HOW TO DECEIVE THE CLEVER LITTLE KNOW-ALL

For most people, there is only one way to lose weight and stay slim, and that is by following the BC Diet. It is the only way out of the maze. A full explanation of my claim is in Chapter 14.

To find your way through the maze, you will have to fool the clever little know-all into thinking that your diet is not a famine. You will then be able to lose weight and stay slim. This trickery has two separate parts. You will need to increase your MR and BMR and reduce your calorie intake. They are both essential. The BC Diet will not work if you reduce your calorie intake without increasing your MR and your BMR.

Evidence that hypothalamic levels can be altered is found when we examine temperature levels. These levels are genetically set in the hypothalamus at 98.6 degrees Fahrenheit. When we feel ill, the first thing a doctor does is take our temperature. This is because a high temperature is a sure sign that we are ill. Microorganisms, such as viruses and bacteria, can, when invading the body, change the level our temperature is set at, proving that it can be moved.

The invasion of microorganisms that raise the set level of temperature from, for example, 98.6 degrees Fahrenheit to 103 degrees Fahrenheit are fooling the clever, little know-all into thinking that the proper body temperature should be 103 degrees Fahrenheit. When our body is invaded by these microorganisms, we begin to shiver and feel cold until our body temperature is exactly 103 degrees Fahrenheit. This level then remains for the duration of the illness.

Our body's defence mechanisms are programmed to fight invading microorganisms at a higher temperature than normal, and, assuming they win, the set temperature will be returned to 98.6 degrees Fahrenheit. When our clever little know-all realises that our temperature is 103 degrees Fahrenheit and should be 98.6 degrees Fahrenheit, he will start lowering it. We will then begin to sweat and feel hot. This is the time when onlookers who have been worried about us say that the fever has broken and that we are going to recover.

If a little virus can alter the genetically programmed temperature level by fooling the clever little know-all, then surely, we should be able to fool him regarding fat levels.

When there is a famine, the clever, little know-all expects to see a reduction in the BMR and the MR at the same time that he sees a reduction in the amount of food that is eaten. If he does, he will know that it is a famine and will activate the starvation response.

If you increase your BMR and the MR at the same time that you reduce the amount of food you eat, the clever, little know-all will not be triggered into action. He will assume that it is not a famine and that everything is all right.

The reason why the clever, little know-all expects to see a fall in the BMR and the MR when there is a famine is because our ancestors would have reduced their physical activities when food was scarce, and their BMR and their MR would have fallen. They would have sat around the fire or huddled in their furs at the back of the cave during a foodless winter. This reaction to a lack of food would have meant a drastic reduction in their BMR and MR. They would not have danced around the fire as they were starving to death.

The human body, after many thousands of years of adapting to foodless winters and famines, reacts in the same way every time there is a shortage of food. This is called the starvation response. We all have this genetic programming. When food intake is reduced, there will be a fall in the BMR and the MR. This fall will tell the clever, little know-all that we are suffering from a famine. If we make sure that our BMR and MR does not fall when we start to lose weight, we will be doing what the virus did; we will be fooling the clever, little know-all.

The starvation response is also triggered by the brain eating the body. I will explain this process later in the book.

If you want to lose weight and stay slim, you must increase your BMR and your MR at the same time that you reduce your calorie intake. In other words, when you start to eat less food, you must increase your BMR and your MR.

Your BMR is the energy (fuel) you use when you are resting or sleeping. It is similar to the petrol that a car uses when the engine is just ticking over. Your MR is a measure of the energy you use during exercise. It can sometimes be high when you are running and sometimes low when you are walking. A car uses fuel in a similar way. The faster a car is driven, the more fuel it uses.

When you go on a diet, there is a reduction in the amount of food (calories) coming into your body. This triggers an automatic reduction in your activity, which reduces your BMR and your MR. The more drastic the diet, the more drastic the fall in the BMR and the MR. This is a genetically programmed response to prevent us from starving to death. The starvation response is found in other animals as well as in humans.

The body reacts to a modern diet in the same way that it reacts to a famine. The fat in the adipose tissue is lost and returned in exactly the same way.

When our ancestors were confronted with a famine, such as a long foodless winter, they would have huddled around the fire or sat in the back of a cave. It was a way of conserving fuel. This lack of activity produced a fall in both the BMR and the MR. Some animals have acquired the ability to reduce their BMR and MR even further when faced with famines or long, foodless winters. Their genetic response is to semi-hibernate or to hibernate. These actions conserve even more fuel.

When you start a weight-reduction diet, you will automatically begin to slow down. You will find that you are walking and moving a lot slower than normal, and you will feel less inclined to engage in any form of exercise. This is not intentional on your part. You will just feel less enthusiastic about physical activities. It is the clever little know-all's way of altering your BMR and MR to conserve fuel.

It is crucial that you prevent your BMR and MR from falling when you start your weight-reduction diet. It will not be easy because the clever, little know-all will be doing all he can to conserve fuel. He will make you feel less inclined to exercise because he regards taking fat out of the body's larder as serious, and he will only do it when he thinks that you are starving to death.

If the clever, little know-all is unable to reduce your BMR and your MR, he will assume that everything is all right and that there is not a famine. The alarm bells will not ring, and he will not take any further action. He will not regard the weight that you lose as life-threatening and will accept the reduced level of weight as your normal body weight. He will then very quickly forget the weight that you used to be.

When you eventually reach your desired size, the clever, little know-all will be unaware that you have lost weight. He will be sitting in the hypothalamus with his feet up, having a snooze. He knows that there has not been a famine; otherwise, your BMR and MR would have fallen. When you start to eat normally again, he will not make you ravenously hungry so that he can replace your fat reserves in preparation for the next famine. He will be happy to accept your new weight as your normal weight. This means that you will not experience the cravings and so will not put the weight you have lost back on. You will stay slim and can forget about dieting. The next chapter will show you how to fool the clever, little know-all.

CHAPTER 4

HOW TO EXERCISE TO INCREASE YOUR METABOLIC RATE AND PREVENT YOUR BASAL METABOLIC RATE FROM FALLING

When you begin reducing the foods you eat, you will need to increase your MR and prevent your BMR from falling. This will be difficult because you will feel less inclined to exercise. You will feel lazy and lethargic. These are the effects of the clever, little know-all trying to conserve fuel. He is trying to switch off a few lights.

You will feel more confident if you plan beforehand exactly what exercises you are going to do. These exercises will have to be in addition to the exercises you already do. You will need to do extra exercises, irrespective of how physical your job is or how many exercises you already do.

You may mow the lawn, do the ironing or vacuum cleaning, etc, but if these activities are already a part of your lifestyle, they will not prevent your MR and BMR from falling. You will need to do additional exercises to the ones you already do.

I will need to risk sounding like a bore and repeat what I have just said, because understanding this point is crucial if the BC Diet is going to work. You must do extra exercises in addition to the exercises you already do. The exercises that you do before you start the BC Diet do not count. They will not increase MR and BMR. You are also advised not to exchange exercises. For example, if you already do tap-dancing, you cannot exchange this exercise for another one as part of this diet. You must maintain your present level of physical activity, as well as do the extra exercises, if you are going to increase your MR and BMR.

You only have to increase your MR and BMR by a small amount. The extra exercises will make sure that your MR and BMR do not fall. The BC Diet will work, and the weight you lose will not return as long as your MR and BMR do not fall.

The exercises you will need to do to prevent your MR and BMR from falling must not be too gentle, such as walking slowly, or too strenuous, such as sprinting. They must be somewhere between these two extremes.

Sprinting uses the oxygen that is in your muscles more quickly than it can be replaced, and an oxygen debt occurs very quickly. Lactic acid will then build up in the muscles, and you will have to stop exercising to repay that oxygen debt by gasping for air, or at least for the oxygen that is in the air. The pain you feel in the muscles when you sprint due to the lack of oxygen is the same sort of pain you get in the heart with angina. This is because the heart is also a muscle, and when the coronary arteries are partially blocked, they prevent blood, which carries oxygen, from reaching the muscle cells, and an oxygen debt builds up.

Exercises that build up an oxygen debt, such as sprinting, are too strenuous and will not induce the correct level of MR and BMR change. Exercises that can be sustained for quite a long time, such as slow walking, are very good for you, but they are not strenuous enough to induce the correct level of MR and BMR change. The exercises you will need to do must be between these two examples. The correct level of exercise, if continued for thirty minutes, should leave you feeling tired, with your muscles aching, and leave you a little out of breath. They should make you pant but not gasp.

The kinds of exercises the average person will need to do are gentle swimming, using a mini-trampoline, slow cycling (using an exercise bike if you want to stay indoors), slow jogging, dancing, ice skating, roller skating, and even brisk walking. If you are young and very fit, then try tennis, badminton, running or even skipping.

You should use about six calories per minute during these exercises. Slow walking only uses about two to three calories per minute and is not strenuous enough, while skipping can use about twelve calories per minute, which, for most people, will be too strenuous.

We are all at different levels of fitness, so any one kind of exercise will affect us all differently. If you are very unfit or a senior citizen, then walking will probably be sufficient. If you are very overweight, you need to be careful not to damage your ankle and knee joints. You would be advised to exercise while sitting or lying down, or go swimming. An exercise bike will enable you to exercise while sitting down and will not put undue pressure on your ankle and knee joints. It is for you to decide what the right level of exercise is for you. The exercise must make you pant but not gasp.

You could use a combination of exercises. For example, you could go to a keep fit class or a gym twice a week (as long as you do not overdo it) and go cycling on the other three days. The only problem with keep-fit classes, the gym, swimming, cycling and jogging, is that they could change your present lifestyle. If you are a busy person and want to keep your lifestyle as it is, you could try exercising at home. You could buy an exercise bike or one of the many exercise machines on sale today. Any form of exercise, as long as it is maintained for at least thirty minutes, will work equally as well.

If you find that you can continue exercising for over an hour, then that level of exercise is not strenuous enough. If you find that you are exhausted and have to stop after ten minutes, then that level of exercise is too strenuous, but if, after thirty minutes, you are out of breath and feel like resting, then that level of exercise is about right for you. The exercises that you decide to do must be done at least five out of every seven days and must last for at least thirty minutes without a break. There is no need to exercise for more than an hour. If you exercise for longer periods of time, you will start to build muscle and feel very hungry, which could result in you eating extra food, so be careful.

These exercises are intended to have a maximum effect in changing your MR and BMR without changing your present lifestyle. If you do not want other members of the family to know that you are on a diet, you could exercise privately in a bedroom. You could even buy an exercise video to make exercising more interesting.

The extra exercises you do when you start reducing the amount of food you eat are not to build muscle; they are to prevent a fall in your MR and BMR.

I am deliberately trying to keep the BC Diet as simple as possible, but this does not mean that it is simple. It would be foolish of me to try to include all the knowledge that has taken me over forty years to assimilate.

The following explanation is for those with an inquisitive mind. The exercises are designed to involve the use of specific muscle fibres. There are slow phasic fibres and fast phasic fibres in our muscles. Fast oxidative fibres use mostly fatty acids (fats) as a fuel to provide movement in a process called oxidative phosphorylation. Whereas fast glycolytic fibres use glucose (sugar) as a fuel to provide movement in a process called glycolysis.

In other words, some exercises (stamina ones such as marathon running) use fat, while others (speed ones such as sprinting) use sugar. If fatty acids are used in our exercises, we will not experience a drop in blood sugar levels (hypoglycaemia), which will stimulate the liver to convert glycogen to glucose (glycogenolysis) and produce very strong hunger pangs.

I do not want to bore you with all the details of my complicated hypothesis, as long as you realise the importance of following my instructions to the letter.

If you are unfit, a senior citizen, or very overweight, it would be better to work up to the required level of exercise very slowly and to consult your doctor before starting the BC Diet. Your doctor is better informed than anyone to know what is best for you.

If, for example, you decide to do jogging as your exercise, do not be tempted to buy a new jogging suit and tell everyone that you will be jogging, especially if you intend to jog where others are jogging. This could encourage you to compete with them and to go faster than you should. Take your time and set your own pace. After all, it is only for thirty minutes each day.

You could start your jogging exercises by walking briskly for thirty minutes each day. Then, when you feel ready, you could jog for short distances during your walk. Eventually, if you feel comfortable, you could jog all the way. But do not force yourself. Take your time. You should enjoy doing your exercises. If you feel uncomfortable in any way, something could be wrong, so stop exercising and consult your doctor.

If you think that running for the bus or the train, in fact, rushing anywhere, will count as part of your exercise, then think again. Your jogging, cycling or walking should be done for fun and not to get you to a particular destination by a particular time. These exercises should not be associated with stress of any kind.

If you are not prepared to exercise for at least thirty minutes on at least five out of every seven days, it will be pointless to lose weight. The BC Diet will not work because the starvation response will be activated, and you will put all the weight you lose back on again. It will be like taking the train to a seaside resort for a day out and being brought back without being allowed to get off the train. It will be a waste of time and effort, to say nothing of the frustration involved.

It is advisable to do a new form of exercise that is not a part of your life and not extend the exercises you already do. Playing golf for an extra thirty minutes or walking the dog for an extra thirty minutes will not work as well as a new exercise. You need to use a new combination of muscles.

CHAPTER 5

HOW TO REDUCE YOUR FOOD INTAKE

Before you start the BC Diet to lose weight, it is important that you think about the size that you intend to be and have at least some idea of how you want to look.

If you have not finished growing, it means that your genes are still in the process of forming your eventual adult shape, so you should be very careful when reducing your calorie intake. Your body will need large amounts of protein and minerals such as calcium for growth. You can cut out all the foods on Lists 1 and 2 (Chapter 8), but foods such as milk, bread, cheese, fish, meat, vegetables, fruit, and a cereal breakfast should be included in your diet each week for a balanced diet.

If you have finished growing up and are now growing out, you will still need protein in your diet as well as minerals such as calcium. Your body's cells are continually dying and need to be replaced. Red blood cells, for instance, last only about 120 days.

In about seven years' time, nearly all of the body you have now will have been replaced by the food you eat. You are what you eat is a very true saying.

It is nice growing up, but not growing out. Carrying your larder around with you is unsightly, unhealthy, and, now that we have the BC Diet, unnecessary. You have probably been tempted to study the many charts that recommend the weight that a person of a particular sex and bone structure should be. You may have even used callipers on your arms and legs to try to measure how much fat you should lose. These methods and BMI (Body Mass Index) are a waste of time. They only leave you feeling confused and worrying about whether you are small, medium, or large-boned. You can forget about the weight that you should be and stop worrying about what size your bones and muscles are. It is what you look like that is important.

Think of yourself as a size and not a weight. And the size you choose should be what you want, not what you think the media or other people want. It is a personal decision.

The first thing you do is to take off all your clothes and stand in front of a full-length mirror. If you think the shock will be too much for the canary, then leave your underwear on. You will need to repeat this procedure once every week throughout your weight-reduction diet (the BC Diet). You will eventually see reflected in your mirror a shape that you can live with, a shape that you are happy with. This is the size that you should be. Your weight is completely irrelevant.

The size you eventually choose will be your personal choice and hopefully not influenced by anyone. You will obviously have to take your age into consideration. If, for instance, you are sixty-five, there will be no need for you to be as slim as you were when you were twenty-one. The days of driving them wild on the beach will have long gone. Anyway, it is nice to cuddle up with someone at night who is not all skin and bone.

It is important to remember that going from fat to slim will probably make you more physically beautiful. At least it will remove some of the fat that is concealing your physical shape. But going from slim to thin will only reduce your physical beauty. It will not make you more beautiful.

There is no need to go too far when losing weight. When you reach an acceptable size, stay that size. It is also worth mentioning that the real true beauty of any human being comes from within the body. This inner beauty is not affected at all by losing weight or by gaining weight. Being fat or thin will not change your inner beauty.

It is more important to be healthy and fit, with sparkling eyes, an alert mind and a good complexion than to be slim. Being a few pounds overweight will not damage your health. Being unfit and on an unbalanced diet will. Do not be too hard on yourself.

You have probably noticed that I do not regard weight as important. The little numbers that appear on your scales when you weigh yourself are only needed to help you lose weight slowly. If someone asks what you weigh, tell them you don’t know and don’t care. It is how we look that is important and not how much we weigh.

If a machine were invented that could reduce a person's weight, say, for example, from 18 stone to 10 stone, would it make them any happier? No, because they would still look the same. They would still look overweight, even though they had lost 8 stone in weight.

When you have reached your desired size, put the scales away or hide them under the bed. You will not need them. Your mirror and clothes will soon tell you if you are putting on weight.

If you are a woman and your thighs and bottom are larger than a man's, there is no need to worry; they should be larger. It is a biological difference that has helped the human race to survive. It is another one of those survival mechanisms.

A woman naturally has more fat on her body than a man, especially around the thighs, bottom and bust. The reason for this extra fat is to help her survive if she becomes pregnant. It is the woman who has to nourish the child as it grows inside her for nine months and who has to breastfeed it for many months after it has been born. It is the woman and not the man who needs the extra fat as a reserve of food in case there is a shortage.

She may not need this extra fat in the same way that her ancestors did, but she is still genetically programmed to possess it. Fat is part of a woman's shape, and it cannot be completely removed. A perfectly shaped woman will have more fat on her body than a man.

A woman will only make herself ill if she tries to lose her womanly shape. It is not natural for a woman to look like a man. She would find it as difficult to lose the fat from her hips and thighs as she would to lose her bust. She is genetically programmed to have large thighs and hips, in the same way that a man is genetically programmed to grow hair on his face. It is this difference between a man and a woman that makes her sexually attractive. A woman should be proud of her womanly shape. A woman's ideal size will always include some fat around the thighs, bottom and bust. There is a great difference between being shapely and being fat. The two are not the same.

The media puts a great deal of pressure on women to be thin and boyish-looking. This size is not only unattractive but also unhealthy. My advice to women is to ignore the trends that dictate their size, especially if they are shapely. Do not assume that all men find thin women attractive; they do not.

The second part of the BC Diet is to reduce the amount of food you eat. If you eat less food, you will have fewer calories to burn, and so you will have less fuel for the body to use. Your body will then have to resort to using the fat that is stored in your adipose tissue.

This sounds very simple, but we must never forget just how clever the little know-all is. He knows exactly where and how much fat you have stored around your body in places you know only too well. He regards that amount as normal for you.

You must reduce your fat levels slowly; otherwise, he will become alarmed and be triggered into action. He will then think that you are starving to death and treat your diet as a famine. For example, if you lose twenty pounds in one month, he will regard it as a famine and make sure that all the weight you have lost is returned.

To decide how much weight you should lose, look at Chapter 13, How Much Weight to Lose Each Week. And remember, it will be far better to lose half a pound per week than to lose more than is recommended per week and run the risk of the clever, little know-all finding out. If you think half a pound in weight is not worth losing, then weigh half a pound of butter. You will then be convinced that half a pound of fat per week is well worth losing.

Modern diets and their promoters are to blame for dieters believing that they have failed if they only lose weight slowly. Worrying about losing too much weight, as opposed to worrying about not losing enough, makes the BC Diet a welcome change.

When I became the guinea pig for the BC Diet, I did jogging as my exercise. To reduce my calorie intake, I stopped eating most of the foods on Food List One (chapter 8) and stopped having sugar in my tea and coffee. I then began to lose a pound to a pound and a half each week. I was still drinking (I like the odd glass of lager), and I was still eating such things as chips, curries, and desserts. When I stopped losing weight, I began to reduce the size of my meals.

It is difficult, confusing, and time-consuming to try to count the calories in the food we eat. My recommendation is to continue eating the same meals you usually do, but reduce their size. If you have three Weetabix for breakfast, reduce it to two. If you have three pieces of bread at lunch time, reduce it to two. And also reduce the size of your main meal.

Before you start the BC Diet, you need to make sure that your body is getting all the nutrients it needs, so make sure you are on a balanced diet before you begin to lose weight.

I can understand you wanting to lose weight quickly; we all do. We are all impatient and have weddings to go to and holidays to look good on, but there is only one way to lose weight and stay slim. There is no shortcut out of the maze. Tell yourself that you are going to look good on the beach next year and not this year. The BC Diet is not a race.

There are many ways you can reduce your calorie intake. One way is to reduce or stop eating the foods that are considered fattening foods, but what are these fattening foods? If you consider sweets and chocolate to be fattening foods, then you are correct because they contain mostly sugar and fat, but it is wrong to consider bread and potatoes as fattening foods; they are nutritionally good foods and contain vitamins, minerals, protein and fibre. It is what you cook the potatoes in and what you spread on the bread that makes them high in calories.

It is important to be careful about the foods you reduce in quantity when trying to lose weight so that you do not become nutritionally deficient. Foods that are safe to cut out completely are those that are similar to the foods that are on List 1 (Chapter 8). These are sweets, cakes and chocolates. They are foods with very little nutritional value and are not to be included as part of your daily nutritional diet. These foods please the mind but not the body. You eat these foods for pleasure and not for their nutritional content.

The foods similar to those on List 2 (Chapter 8) are good for you, but they are very high in calories and contain large amounts of fat and sugar. These are the sorts of foods that you can reduce in quantity when you are trying to lose weight on the BC Diet. They can even be cut out completely when trying to lose weight. They are foods that please the mind and not the body.

It is important that you do not start the BC Diet by cutting out too many foods; otherwise, you will lose weight too quickly. You must cut them out gradually so that you lose weight slowly. You must also allow about a month between any previous diet and starting the BC Diet. This will allow time for your body weight to level out at your normal weight. You do not want the effects of your last diet to spoil the effects of the BC Diet.

You must now start the BC Diet; that is, you start exercising and reducing your food intake. The first step is to stop having sugar in your tea and coffee.

On the first day of your diet, you must weigh yourself and write down your weight. You must always weigh yourself at the same time, i.e., before breakfast, on the same day of the week, and wearing the same clothes. You must not weigh yourself again for a full seven days. It is tempting to keep weighing yourself during the week just to see how much weight you have lost, but this will only confuse you. You need to be patient. The BC Diet cannot be rushed. After seven days, weigh yourself again and write down your weight. What you do next depends on one of the following: A, B or C.

A. If you have lost too much weight, you will need to eat a little more food.

B. If you do not lose enough weight, you will need to eat a little less food.

C. If you have lost the correct amount of weight, continue to eat the same amount of food.

If you are losing too much weight, then treat yourself, but do not return to the bad habit of having sugar in your tea and coffee. You will find that, in time, you will enjoy your tea and coffee just as much without sugar as you did with it. Do not try to reduce the amount of sugar you have in your tea and coffee. It will only prolong the agony. Stop it completely. It will taste awful at first, but keep drinking it. You will eventually find that your tea and coffee will taste as good as it ever did.

The foods on List 1 that contain large amounts of sugar and fat are foods that feed the mind. If you eat these foods as well as having sugar in your tea and coffee, you will eventually suffer the consequences. Your body has not been designed to work on large amounts of sugar and fat.

When you start the BC Diet, the main thing to remember is to start your exercises at the same time that you begin to reduce the number of calories you eat. The word calorie may confuse you, but it is just a measure of the energy value of our food, just as a metre is a measure of distance. Calories are found in all forms of food. If we eat more calories than we need, we put on weight, but if we eat fewer calories than we need, we lose weight.

You may be surprised to know that sugar and protein, as well as fat, can be converted to fat and stored in the adipose tissue. It does not matter what you eat; if it is more than your body needs, it will be converted to fat and stored away as a reserve fuel in your adipose tissue. The body breaks down the molecular structure of the foods we eat and makes what it needs from them.

Protein is broken down into amino acids to make human protein in the same way that a builder can demolish a block of flats and make a cowshed, a shop, and three houses out of bricks. If we eat more protein than our body needs, it will be broken down and used for energy or converted into fat and stored in our adipose tissue.

All the carbohydrates and sugar we eat are broken down and converted to glucose. This sugar floats around in our blood and is either used by our cells as fuel, converted to glycogen and stored in our liver and muscles, or converted to fat and stored in our adipose tissue.

To lose weight, you need to reduce the sugar and fat content of your food. You could stop having sugar in your tea and coffee, use low-calorie ketchup and salad dressings, and have low-calorie drinks. This approach to reducing sugar in your diet does not deprive you of tea, coffee, ketchup, or soft drinks. Fat can be reduced in your diet by taking the skin off chicken, not using fat from the meat in the gravy, having low-fat cheese and yoghurt, using low-fat skimmed milk in your tea and coffee, cutting the fat off meat, poaching, boiling and grilling food; buying processed foods that have a reduced level of fat, and by spreading the margarine or butter on sandwiches less generously.

Besides being high in calories, there is a more sinister side to fat that is causing a great deal of concern. Fat is blamed for causing many diseases, but because it is a very complicated substance and exists in many different forms, its exact effect on the body is still unclear.

Because a high level of cholesterol in the blood is associated with atherosclerosis, you may decide to cut out all the foods in your diet containing cholesterol. You may think that this form of action will reduce the level of cholesterol in your blood and improve your health. It is not as simple as that. Your liver can make cholesterol from the other foods that you eat, so reducing cholesterol in your diet may stimulate the liver to make more cholesterol. This is because cholesterol is an essential substance needed by the body to make things such as cell membranes, myelin sheaths for nerves, bile, and hormones.

Evidence suggests that it is the saturated fat in our diet and not cholesterol that is to blame for these fat-related diseases. My advice is not to worry about the cholesterol content of your food but to reduce the amount of saturated fats in your diet. Saturated fats come mostly from animals and set hard at room temperature, such as lard and suet. Unsaturated fats (the less harmful kind) remain as a liquid at room temperature. We call these fats oils.

Use polyunsaturated oil in your diet for putting on salads, but use monounsaturated oil for frying. Polyunsaturated oils such as olive oil, when heated, break down into aldehydes and are believed to be harmful.

You do not need saturated fats in your diet because the essential fatty acids (EFAs) are polyunsaturated. EFAs (once called vitamin F) are linoleic and linolenic acid. They are found in salmon, mackerel, walnuts, pistachios, vegetables and whole eggs. EFAs are only needed by the body in very small amounts. Linolenic acid is sometimes called Omega 3.

To reduce the saturated fats in your diet, you could read the content lists of foods for the hidden saturated fats. Saturated fats are usually high in foods such as sausages, meat pies, mincemeat, cakes, ice cream, cream, chocolate, black pudding, pastry, pork pies, biscuits, etc. Eating less red meat and eating more fish and poultry will also help to reduce saturated fat in your diet.

CHAPTER 6

THE TIME IT SHOULD TAKE FOR YOU TO LOSE WEIGHT

These recommendations are not to be taken too literally. They are to be used as a general guide to help you lose weight slowly so that you do not alarm the clever, little know-all.

If you want to lose a total of 7 lbs, you should lose 1½lbs per week, which should take you 5 weeks.

If you want to lose 1st, you should lose 2lbs per week, which should take about 7 weeks.

If you want to lose 2st, you should lose 2½lbs per week, which should take about 12 weeks.

If you want to lose 3st or more, lose 3lbs per week until you have 2st to lose, then lose 2½lbs per week

The general rule is that the nearer you get to your desired size, the slower the weight loss should be. Do not worry if you remain at the same weight for a while. It is normal to have good and bad weeks. You do not lose weight in the same way that sand falls through an egg timer. Weight loss is a little erratic, so be patient. The longer your diet takes, the more time the clever, little know-all will have to accept your new weight as your normal weight. To find out the maximum weight that you can safely lose per week, look at Chapter 13, How Much Weight to Lose Each Week.

CHAPTER 7

RECOMMENDED FOODS TO SUPPLY ALL OF YOUR NUTRITIONAL NEEDS

We all use the word diet to mean that we are trying to lose weight, although it should be used to describe the food we eat. A balanced diet is a combination of foods that contain all the nutrients we need for a healthy body.

Many dieters who have been trying to lose weight for years and who have tried diet after diet but who are still overweight get depressed at the mere thought of a diet. Most of their enjoyment of food has gone. They now regard food as a threat to their happiness and health, especially the foods that taste good. They believe that if a food tastes good, it must be bad for them, and they feel guilty if they indulge in these bad foods. It is much easier on their conscience to nibble on a carrot or a lettuce leaf. What a sad state the world of dieting has become.

Food is a wonderful array of tasty substances. They are there to be enjoyed, and we should be able to eat all of the foods we desire. The mouth-watering anticipation of a meal, an ice cream, or even a cream cake should be a part of everyone's life. Food should not run hand-in-hand with guilt. When we think of food, we should think of pleasure and happiness.

One of the saddest articles I have ever read was about a woman who followed a diet that contained large amounts of shark. She was, unfortunately, unaware that sharks are carnivores and at the top of the food chain. When small organisms are contaminated or eat contaminated food, the contaminants, such as mercury, accumulate when they are eaten by larger animals, who are, in turn, eaten by even larger animals. Eventually, these contaminated animals are eaten by animals at the top of the food chain, whose bodies store the contaminant. The woman in question, who regarded herself as an expert on nutrition, eventually suffered from brain damage due to mercury poisoning.

You need, arguably, thirteen different vitamins, twenty-six minerals, twenty amino acids, essential fatty acids, carbohydrates, water and fibre in your diet. It is very complicated, and unless you make it your life's work, you will only get confused when studying nutrition. Forget about going on the internet for information on human nutritional needs, and instead, remember the words variety and moderation. They are very important words. If you remember that variety and moderation apply to all the foods you eat (fruit, vegetables, meat, etc.), you will make it difficult for a nutritional deficiency to raise its ugly head.

Vitamin absorption into the body (bioavailability) varies from person to person and can be affected by drugs or illnesses such as diarrhoea. The bioavailability of vitamins can be affected by minerals, other vitamins, and the amount of specific proteins produced by the body. For example, vitamin B12 requires an intrinsic factor to enable it to be absorbed into the body. The amount of B12 absorbed will depend on the amount of the intrinsic factor released into the stomach. Calcium needs vitamin D before it can be absorbed into the body, and vitamin A's absorption is reduced by liquid paraffin and enhanced by lipids (fats).

The intellectual mind of modern man still has a great deal to learn about human nutrition, whereas his body knows all there is to know. The body will simply take all the nutrients it needs from the food that is eaten. All we have to do is make sure that we eat sufficient amounts of these foods.

It is easy to get carried away and become over-concerned with, for instance, vitamin A. You could then run the risk of suffering from vitamin A poisoning. You may start eating large amounts of liver, knowing that it contains high levels of vitamin A, but this could be harmful. We should only eat liver about once a week, and pregnant women should not eat it at all. If we take high levels of any one vitamin or mineral, it will disrupt the balance of the body and could cause a deficiency in other vitamins and minerals.

It may interest you to know that you could die from vitamin A poisoning by eating polar bear liver. Several explorers of years ago did. The polar bear is a carnivore at the top of a food chain and accumulates vitamin A in its liver by eating seals that have eaten large amounts of vitamin A-rich fish. Eskimos bury polar bear liver to prevent their dogs from eating it.

There is no need to take vitamin or mineral supplements in your diet, although you could take a vitamin C tablet and a multivitamin and mineral tablet each day when you are ill or when you are trying to lose weight on the BC Diet.

There is one food that can be cut out when you are trying to lose weight, and that is sugar. Sugar is only used as fuel by the body and contains no other nutrients. There is more than enough natural sugar in our normal diet to provide all the fuel we need. The only problem is, sugar is usually present in large amounts in the foods that we eat for pleasure. These are the foods that feed the mind and so will be needed as an occasional treat, even when you are trying to lose weight.

You also need fibre in your diet, so have a cereal breakfast with milk on at least four out of every seven days. I recommend a cereal breakfast because it contains the right kind of fibre. Also have wholemeal bread. White bread only contains about half the fibre of wholemeal bread. Have fresh fruit and raw vegetables every day. Have at least four different kinds of fresh fruit and four different kinds of raw vegetables each week.

Have one of these six high-protein foods every day: chicken, turkey, fish, eggs, cheese and red meat. Include at least four of these six foods in your diet on a weekly basis. Have three different kinds of cooked vegetables with your meal, and include at least six different kinds of vegetables per week. Have oily fish as well as non-oily fish each week. Oily fish are salmon, mackerel, herring, sardines and pilchards. Non-oily fish are cod, haddock, plaice, coley, whiting and halibut.

Nuts provide a high level of protein and many different minerals. They are very good for you, but they also contain a large amount of fat, so be careful when trying to lose weight. Pasta, such as macaroni, spaghetti, vermicelli, cannelloni, ravioli, lasagne, etc, are made from flour and can be regarded as unfortified bread in your diet. The foods added to them or eaten with them are often high in calories and could be reduced when trying to lose weight.

Tinned foods such as baked beans or peas are good for you, but often contain chemicals and added salt, so be careful. If, for instance, you have a meal of meat and three veg, it would be advisable to have only one of the vegetables out of a tin.

If you follow the above suggestions, you will not have to worry about unfamiliar words such as amino acids, proteins, carbohydrates, monosaccharides, glycerol, fatty acids, enzymes, and nucleic acids, to name but a few.

Oxalic acid is found in fruits and vegetables such as strawberries, rhubarb, green tomatoes, and spinach and can join with calcium to form oxalate, an insoluble compound that cannot be absorbed into the body. This does not mean that you have to stop eating strawberries, rhubarb, or spinach as long as you remember the word variety. Large amounts of any one kind of food will eventually be harmful. I personally have a soft spot for rhubarb and custard.

Phytic acid is found in most plant materials, especially in the outer layers of cereals, and can also form insoluble compounds with calcium, as well as with copper, iron and zinc, preventing these materials from being used by the body. Phytic acid is partly destroyed by the action of yeast, such as in the baking of bread. Many scientists now believe that phytic acid is harmless because the body can adapt to it.

There are substances such as goitrogens that are found in foods such as cabbage and kale leaves, mustard and rapeseeds, and cassava and soya beans. They can reduce iodine absorption in the body and cause goitre. But again, there is no need to worry. Cooking tends to destroy goitrogens, and because you do not live on the above-mentioned foods alone, you will not get goitre. Variety in our diet helps prevent many diseases.

Many frightening substances occur naturally in our food, even small amounts of poisons such as arsenic, but the body has, over many thousands of years, adapted to them and can render them harmless. That is, as long as we do not live on a very small variety of foods. The smaller the variety of foods in our diet, the higher the chance that these substances will cause problems.

There are thirteen vitamins and almost a hundred naturally occurring minerals, making it extremely difficult for science to ascertain their effects on each other while they are inside the human body. If we were small enough to float about in the blood, we would find hundreds of different molecules and compounds interacting with each other. We would find red blood cells carrying oxygen to every cell of the body. There would be many different kinds of white blood cells (the body's defence system) that seek out and destroy foreign particles. There would be platelets that help in blood clotting, twenty different amino acids, glucose, fats, hormones, enzymes, nucleic acids, etc. Mixed up in this soup of ingredients, there would also be the many different vitamins and minerals that are absorbed from the food we eat.

The human body will cope with all the different ingredients in its blood, as long as they are not too extreme, and will make (synthesise) all manner of enzymes, cells, hormones, etc. All that you need to do is supply it with the raw materials. This is, and I do not apologise for repeating myself, why variety is so important. Variety is the spice of life.

We are all aware that we have a body that needs nourishment, although we sometimes forget that we also have a mind. The mind also needs to be fed. The nutritional needs of the body are extremely complicated, but the nutritional needs of the mind are very simple. You just feed the mind what it wants. If, for instance, you like chocolate, sausages and cream cakes, then eat them. Not necessarily at the same time, but always include in your diet the foods that you enjoy.

You may gain weight if you eat too many of your favourite foods, which usually contain fat and sugar, so you will need to balance them in your diet. You could, for example, have a bar of chocolate on Monday, a cream cake on Wednesday, and chips on Sunday. As long as you are on a balanced diet, you can confidently eat the so-called junk foods.

Even though a food may be nutritionally empty and contain only calories, it can still be good for you. This, at first, may seem to be a contradictory statement, but it makes sense when you consider the mind. The mind and body work as a team. They may be separate, but they are intimately connected. Whatever pleases the mind will also please the body, and vice versa. If you look forward to a cream cake on a Wednesday afternoon, it will do you good physically by making you feel happy. A happy body functions better than an unhappy one. Making yourself unhappy and depressed by not eating the foods that you would like to eat will only make your body function less well.

The cereal breakfast, wholemeal bread, vegetables and fruit in your diet will supply all the fibre you need. You may not regard fibre as essential, but you would die without it. Fibre stimulates defecation and helps remove waste products before they are broken down into harmful substances. A lack of fibre is believed to cause or contribute to diseases such as irritable bowel syndrome, constipation, diverticulosis, appendicitis and colonic cancer. Fibre also provides food for the bacteria that live in your gut that synthesise (make) some vitamins and fatty acids. Because these vitamins and fatty acids are absorbed into the body, fibre could be regarded as food. All the vitamin K you need is supplied by these bacteria.

You may wonder what part alcohol plays in a diet. Alcohol is a food, and when drunk, it is broken down by the liver. Part of the alcohol will be used as fuel, and the rest will be converted into fat. You must treat alcoholic drinks in the same way you treat the foods on List 1. Alcohol is food for the mind and should be regarded as a treat.

CHAPTER 8

FOOD LISTS

LIST 1

These are examples of foods that are only eaten for pleasure and not for their nutritional value. They contain mostly empty calories.

CHOCOLATE. SYRUP. SWEETS. HONEY. CAKES. ALCOHOL. ICE CREAM. KETCHUP. ICE LOLLIES. SALAD CREAM. CREAM. SUGAR. BISCUITS. CRISPS. SCRATCHINGS. SOFT DRINKS. CORDIAL. JELLIES. TARTS. JAM. MARMALADE.

LIST 2

These are examples of foods that are nutritionally good for you but also contain large amounts of sugar, salt and fat.

CHIPS. TRIFLE. TINNED MEAT. SAUSAGES. ROAST POTATOES. TINNED FRUIT. TINNED VEGETABLES. PIES. MINCEMEAT. DESERTS. BUTTER. PASTIES. PIGS PUDDING. BURGERS. PIZZAS. TV DINNERS. PASTRY. PANCAKES. FRIED BREAD. FRIED RICE. MAYONNAISE. PEANUT BUTTER.

CHAPTER 9

BODY-CONTROLLED DIET AT A GLANCE

This condensed information about the BC Diet is not intended to be a substitute for reading the BC Diet book. It would be helpful if you read the book first and use this chapter to refresh your memory.

1. Start the BC Diet by reducing your calorie intake.
2. Start your exercises at the same time that you reduce your calorie intake. These exercises must be continued without a break for at least 30 minutes and on a minimum of 5 out of every 7 days. You must pant but not gasp. There is no need to do the exercises for more than 60 minutes, and you only need to do them once a day. (Chapter 4)
3. Only lose weight slowly (Chapter 6 and Chapter 13)
4. You can cut down or cut out completely the kinds of foods on Lists 1 and 2 (Chapter 8) but do not cut out completely any of the foods that should be a part of your balanced daily diet, such as cereals, milk, bread, margarine (or butter), fruit, vegetables, and the main six protein foods, chicken, turkey, fish, eggs, cheese and red meat. These foods can be reduced, but they should not be cut out completely.
5. If you lose weight too quickly, you must treat yourself by eating something extra during the following

week, such as a cake, a chocolate bar or an extra portion of your favourite food; the choice is yours.

6. While trying to lose weight, have one vitamin C tablet and one multivitamin and mineral tablet each day.

CHAPTER 10

A WIDER VIEW OF NUTRITION, PLUS USEFUL TIPS AND INFORMATION

Modern man has changed his diet over the past hundred years or so in a most drastic way and is now suffering the consequences. There is no need for us to return to the lifestyle of a hunter-gatherer and resort to living in caves. We do not have to change our lifestyle, but we do have to change our diet. We need to eat the foods our bodies are programmed to eat so they will work at their best. If a car is designed to use petrol as fuel, it will work less well if diesel is put into its tank.

We cannot redesign or reprogram our bodies. Any change that does take place occurs over many, many years. A thousand years is a very short time when dealing with evolutionary change.

Human ear muscles are a good example of how slow evolutionary change is. We all still possess ear muscles that were once used to home in on sound, but only a few of us can use them. We also possess an appendix, although it is now very small. In time, these vestigial remnants will vanish altogether, and we will not be able to move our ears or eat the foods that the appendix once catered for. Our bodies do change over time, but only very slowly, and not fast enough to cope with the drastic changes in our modern diet, which now contains very large amounts of sugar, fat, and salt.

We are genetically programmed to produce enzymes that break down our food so it can be used by the body. There are thousands of different enzymes, but they are all highly specific and perform only one job in one particular way. Enzymes are proteins and sometimes work with co-enzymes, such as vitamins, to catalyse chemical reactions.

The DNA in our cells unzips and serves as a template or pattern to pass on the inherited information specifying the exact composition of a protein, such as an enzyme. These copies are exact and can only follow the original plan that is in the genes (the DNA helix). If we do not provide the correct amount of amino acids needed to make the protein, the protein cannot be made.

The protein foods we eat, such as meat, bread, cheese, fish, etc., are broken down to make human protein. We need all 20 amino acids to make the different kinds of proteins the human body needs, such as muscle, enzymes, and keratin (which is found in hair and nails). The plan in the DNA (in our genes) cannot be changed to make a new protein. If the body cannot follow the original plan, it will not make that particular protein, at least not a functioning one. We could then suffer from a protein deficiency.

If you follow a balanced diet, you will provide your body with all the amino acids it needs.

Our diet must contain thirteen different vitamins if we are to remain healthy. Vitamins (to be scientifically correct, are called micronutrients) are not used as a fuel for energy, like sugar, or as building blocks, like protein, but to help in a variety of metabolic reactions that are essential to life.

The thirteen vitamins that you need are:

VITAMIN A. RETINOL.

Retinol is a fat-soluble vitamin that is found only in foods from animals. It is found in foods such as fish oil, liver, margarine, butter, cheese and eggs. It can be stored in the body (in the liver) for about two years. Carotene, which is found in fruits and vegetables, can be converted into retinol by the body. The dark green leaves of vegetables, such as cabbage, contain more carotene than the pale green leaves. Carotene cannot be absorbed into the body unless fat has been eaten at the same time. If large amounts of vitamin A are eaten, it could be very dangerous and could even kill you because it cannot be excreted by the body.

VITAMIN Bl. THIAMINE.

Thiamine is a water-soluble vitamin that is found in foods such as meat (especially pork), milk, fish, eggs, liver, bread, cereals, fruit and vegetables. All water-soluble vitamins leech into the water when food is being cooked, especially vitamin B1 and vitamin C. You can recover the lost vitamins by using the water that the food was cooked in, in the gravy. Sugar, fats and alcohol contain no thiamine.

VITAMIN B2. RIBOFLAVIN.

Riboflavin is a water-soluble vitamin found in foods such as liver, cheese, eggs, meat, milk and breakfast cereals.

VITAMIN B6. PYRIDOXINE.

Pyridoxine is a water-soluble vitamin found in foods such as meat, fish, fruit, vegetables, bread, milk and cereal bran. Extra supplements in tablet form can be dangerous.

VITAMIN B12. CYANOCOBALAMIN.

Cyanocobalamin is a water-soluble vitamin found in foods such as liver, fish, meat, eggs, cheese and breakfast cereals. It can be stored in the liver for about three years.

FOLIC ACID.

Folic acid is a water-soluble vitamin found in foods such as liver, green leafy vegetables, eggs, breakfast cereals and citrus fruits.

NICOTINIC ACID. Also called NIACIN.

Nicotinic acid is a water-soluble vitamin found in foods such as meat, liver, cheese, fish, bread, breakfast cereals, eggs, milk and vegetables. The amino acid tryptophan can be converted to nicotinic acid by the body.

PANTOTHENIC ACID.

Pantothenic acid is a water-soluble vitamin found in almost every sort of food.

BIOTIN.

Biotin is a water-soluble vitamin found in a wide variety of foods. It may not be needed in our diet because the small amounts that we do need are made by the bacteria in our large intestine. Egg yolk that is cooked is rich in bioavailable biotin, but raw egg white contains avidin, which makes biotin unavailable to the body.

VITAMIN C. ASCORBIC ACID.

Ascorbic acid is a water-soluble vitamin found in foods such as fruit and vegetables, although not in cereal grains. A vitamin C tablet or a small glass of pure fruit juice can be taken each day when losing weight, during an illness, or after an injury. The only mammals that need vitamin C in their diet are the primates (which include humans), the fruit bat, and the guinea pig.

VITAMIN E. TOCOPHEROL.

Tocopherol is a fat-soluble vitamin found in most foods, especially the oils of wheat germ, soybean, maize, and sunflower. It is also found in foods such as green leafy vegetables, meat and fruit. It can be stored in the body.

VITAMIN K. PHYLLOQUINONE.

Phylloquinone is a fat-soluble vitamin found in foods such as vegetables, liver and meat. It is synthesised by gut bacteria and is probably not needed in our diet. Newborn babies whose intestines are sterile at birth and so do not contain bacteria may, in the first few days of life, suffer from a blood-clotting problem. This can be rectified by an injection of vitamin K. A long course of antibiotics could kill the bacteria in the gut of an adult, and so could cause a vitamin K deficiency.

VITAMIN D. CALCIFEROL.

Calciferol is a fat-soluble vitamin found in foods such as fish, eggs, margarine, butter, milk, liver and breakfast cereals. A precursor in the skin can be converted to vitamin D by the action of ultraviolet radiation in sunlight. The melanin in the skin of dark-skinned people prevents some ultraviolet radiation from penetrating, and so less vitamin D is synthesised. Vitamin D is the most toxic of the vitamins. Large amounts can cause more calcium to be absorbed than can be excreted, resulting in kidney damage. Calciferol can be stored in the liver. Vitamin D is now regarded as a hormone.

There are eight major minerals (elements) that must be included in our diet, and a further nine trace elements that are needed in very small amounts. A further nine minerals may be needed. If there is a deficiency in the UK, it is usually iron, iodine or calcium.

The eight major minerals are:

IRON.

Iron is found in foods such as liver, meat, eggs, fish, bread and breakfast cereals. Iron is not absorbed into the body at the same rate from all foods. About 40% of iron is absorbed from meat, fish and poultry, but only about 10% from eggs, whole grains, nuts and dried beans. Only about 2% of the iron in spinach is absorbed. Deficiency can arise from losing blood due to an accident or from extra-heavy periods. Menstruating women will not normally need extra iron. Consult your doctor before taking any mineral supplements. Iron can be stored in the liver, spleen, bone marrow and muscles.

CALCIUM.

Calcium is found in foods such as cheese, milk, bread, tinned fish with the bones, nuts and pulses such as peas, beans and lentils.

PHOSPHORUS.

Phosphorus is found in nearly all foods. A deficiency has not been found in humans.

MAGNESIUM.

Magnesium is widespread in foods.

SODIUM/CHLORINE.

Sodium chlorine is found in most foods as sodium chloride (common salt). High intakes of salt have been associated with high blood pressure, so it should not be added to your food after it has been cooked. Salt should never be added to an infant's diet because their kidneys cannot excrete the excess.

POTASSIUM.

Potassium is widespread in foods.

SULPHUR.

Sulphur is widespread in foods. Supplied mostly by the protein in our diet. There is no evidence of a deficiency being found in animals or humans.

Trace elements are only needed in very small amounts. They are:

COBALT.

Cobalt is found in a wide variety of foods. A deficiency has not been found in humans, only in sheep. It is part of vitamin B12, hence the name cyanocobalamin.

CHROMIUM.

Chromium is found in a wide variety of foods. A deficiency is rare.

FLUORINE.

Fluorine is found in drinking water, tea, seafood and in fish if the bones are eaten.

MANGANESE.

Manganese is found in a wide variety of foods. It is also found in tea.

IODINE.

Iodine is found in fish, seafood, vegetables and cereals. The iodine content of vegetables and cereals depends on the iodine content of the soil they grew in. The iodine content of foods from animals depends on the iodine content of the animal's diet. There is widespread use of iodides in animal feed, so meat, eggs, and especially milk, are useful sources of iodine.

SELENIUM.

Selenium is found in a wide variety of foods. A deficiency is rare.

ZINC.

Zinc is found in most foods, especially in association with protein. A deficiency is very rare.

COPPER.

Copper is found in a wide variety of foods. A deficiency is very rare.

MOLYBDENUM.

Molybdenum is found in a wide variety of foods. A deficiency is very rare.

The human body may also need the following nine minerals. They are present in the body in very small amounts. SILICON. NIOBIUM. SCANDIUM. THALLIUM. VANADIUM. BORON. TIN. NICKEL. ARSENIC.

If you have read the official booklet on 'E' numbers, you will probably feel that they are good for you and very necessary. That is the intention of the booklet. The booklet, I am sorry to say, gives a very one-sided account. To get the full story, you must get advice from an independent source. There are many nutritional experts who are very concerned about 'E' numbers that are being put into our food.

'E' numbers are chemicals that are added to our food to give it extra colour, body, texture, taste, or to preserve it. Some chemicals are necessary in our modern society, such as those that preserve food, but others, such as those that add colour to food, are unnecessary. It would not be so important if we could be sure that all the chemicals that are used as 'E' numbers are harmless, but we cannot be sure. You can imagine the harm that could be done by adding chemicals to the many different ingredients that are already floating around in our blood.

Nearly all of the foods we eat contain 'E' numbers, and they can accumulate in our bodies to dangerous levels. Even medically prescribed drugs and tablets are frequently coloured with E102 (tartrazine). Those in support of putting these chemicals into our food will argue that they are harmless. They will say, for instance, that E150 is only burnt sugar called caramel, but there are many ways that the sugar or carbohydrate can be burnt. Caramel produced by ammonia acting as the burning agent on carbohydrate has been shown to cause vitamin B6 deficiency in rats. This example shows the complexity of ‘E’ numbers.

My advice is not to study chemicals and their effects on food, but to avoid all 'E' numbers if possible. Select the foods that contain the least amount of 'E' numbers. Food manufacturers are now aware that the public is looking for 'E' numbers, so they sometimes put the name of the chemical instead of the 'E' number on their products. For example, they put caramel instead of E150. You need to look at the list of ingredients, and if it contains strange-sounding names such as amaranth, sulphites, or sorbitol, these will be the 'E' numbers. There is no need to become fanatical about 'E' numbers, but take special care when buying foods for pregnant women and children.

Many of the artificial colours that are used in foods are unnecessary. I am sure we could get used to eating tinned peas that are not bright green. Do not automatically classify all 'E' numbers as harmful. Some, for instance, are vitamins. E101 is vitamin B2, E306 is vitamin E, E375 is nicotinic acid, E300 is vitamin C, and El60 is carotene.

If you reach for the toffee jar or the biscuit tin when you feel depressed or anxious, do not feel you are a failure. Most of us use food as a source of comfort. This is because when we have eaten, we not only feel full, we also feel satisfied, relaxed, and less anxious. There is a biological need to feed the mind as well as the body, and delicious-tasting foods not only act as a source of pleasure but can, on occasion, act as a crutch to help us through times of anxiety and depression.

The danger of eating your favourite foods when you feel low is that you may gain weight due to the high-calorie content of these foods. This, of course, depends on how often you get depressed. If you find that you are overweight because of long bouts of depression or anxiety, then you will need to seek professional help and advice. Do not suffer in silence. Go to see your doctor. He or she will be only too pleased to help you.

Do not be ashamed of being mentally ill or of having a mental problem. You expect to become physically ill at times because you have a body, so you must also expect at some time during your life to become mentally ill because you also have a mind. It would be much better to sort out any emotional problems before trying to lose weight.

I have explained the exercises you need to do to lose weight and stay slim, but you also need physical activity even when you are not trying to lose weight. Our bodies are programmed to expect a physically energetic existence, and although some of us do have physically taxing occupations, most of us do not. Most of us spend a large part of every day sitting down. We drive the car to work, where we sit down, and when we return home, we sit down to watch television. We are using our bodies less than they should be used.

Until about a hundred years ago, nearly everyone led a physically demanding life. Almost from birth, they walked everywhere and worked physically hard. There were no schools or old people's homes, and no jobs where they could sit down all day. The jobs they did were all physical, such as a blacksmith, soldier, thatcher, builder, farmer, stonemason, woodcutter, etc. And the further back in time you go, the more physically demanding life becomes. We have almost made our bodies redundant by allowing machines to do all the hard work for us. They carry us about, wash our clothes, cook for us, and even entertain us. If we expect our bodies not to malfunction, we must make some sort of effort.

There is no need to go from one extreme to the other and suddenly start playing strenuous sports like squash or running marathons. Foolishness like that could cost you your life. Your exercises should be gentle at first, gradually building up to a level that suits your age and lifestyle. You could improve your health and probably extend your life by walking more often and using the stairs instead of the lift.

If you are a keen gardener or engage in sports such as golf, you probably exercise enough, but if in your heart of hearts, you feel that you do not exercise enough, then at least walk more often. Walking for pleasure is an extremely good exercise for both mind and body.

Having a nutritionally balanced diet is not good enough on its own. You also need to be fit if you want to be healthy. If you become ill, and you will one day, your body will put up a better fight if it is in tip-top condition. If you are overweight, on an unbalanced diet, or unfit, your body will not be able to put up as good a fight as it should. It is a battle that you can only lose once. Make an effort to get fit and keep fit.

Many of the books on nutrition are fanatical in their views and make outrageous statements, such as denouncing all processed food as poisonous and that saturated fat and sugar should not be eaten at all, even to the point of depriving children of sweets. We are all concerned about what we should eat, but there is no need to become fanatical. I recommend eating wholemeal bread as part of The Recommended Daily Diet, but this does not mean that I regard white bread as bad for you. White bread is also very good for you, although it does not contain as much roughage (fibre) as wholemeal bread.

It is important to understand that although foods such as chocolate and cakes contain large amounts of saturated fats and sugar and can damage your health if eaten in excess, they are still an important part of your diet. They are the cherry on the cake. If you cut them out completely, it could do more harm to the mind and, hence, to the body than eating too many of them. They must be a balanced part of your diet in the same way that alcohol and other foods for the mind are. Instead of becoming fanatical, be reasonable. The word to remember when eating foods for the mind is moderation.

A clue about what we should eat can be found in what the people of the UK had to eat during the Second World War. It was a time of intense stress for the population due to the loss of the young men who were fighting abroad, and from the continual bombing, but even though it was a terrible time, the population emerged from the war healthier than before. Their diet during the war contained less fat, sugar, salt, and meat, and more fruit, vegetables, and fibre. They had wholemeal bread and less processed foods. Even the number of people suffering from heart disease fell during and just after the war.

Eating the foods that you like; that's living. Putting on weight from eating too much; that's life.

The decision to become a vegetarian is personal and for you alone to make, but you will have to take special care that your decision does not harm your health. A vegetarian diet, if carefully planned, will provide sufficient nutrients, especially if it includes milk, cheese and eggs. Vegans, on the other hand, who do not eat any foods of animal origin, will find it more difficult.

Vegetarians will need a wide variety of cereals, peas, beans, nuts, and bread to provide them with sufficient protein, and will need to ensure their diet contains sufficient zinc, calcium, iron, riboflavin, vitamin D, and vitamin B12.

Pregnancy can put an enormous strain on the body, and a vegan has to be extra careful to make sure that they eat sufficient nutrients to supply the growing baby. The breast milk of strict vegetarian mothers can be deficient in vitamins and minerals. The reason why vegans need to take special care is because the human body, over millions of years, has adapted to a diet that contains some meat. To change from an omnivorous to an herbivorous diet is asking a great deal of your body's adaptability. It will need some help from you. Make sure your diet is adequate well before trying to conceive, and consult a doctor before taking vitamin and mineral supplements.

A vegetarian reduces the variety of foods in their diet and could suffer from a minor deficiency. When they become ill or suffer from long periods of stress, it puts a strain on their body's resources. The amino acids, vitamins, minerals, and EFAs will still be floating around in their blood or stored in their body, but some of them could become reduced in numbers. A cell, for instance, that is synthesising enzymes or hormones may not be able to obtain a particular amino acid or vitamin as quickly as it would like. It is the same as reducing the number of buses in a city. The public will still be able to get a bus, but they will have to wait longer for it to arrive.

Vitamin B12 deficiency occurs relatively frequently in the UK, but is caused more often than not by a lack of the intrinsic factor and not from a lack of vitamin B12 in the diet. The intrinsic factor is a protein made by the body and is needed before vitamin B12 (the extrinsic factor) can be absorbed.

These are twenty snippets of information from the experts.

1. Eating raw fish can reduce thiamine levels in the body by up to 50%.
2. Synthetic vitamins are as good as natural ones. Chemically, the two are the same.
3. The minerals from sea salt are insignificant and have no beneficial effect. The same is true of the vitamin and mineral content of brown sugar and honey. You would have to eat enormous amounts for them to be of any nutritional value.
4. Kelp has no special food value other than high levels of iodine and should not be eaten by pregnant women.
5. Wine manufacturers are permitted to put up to 70 additives and any amount of sulfur dioxide into their wine.
6. There are up to 50 permitted additives that can be put into beer, including seaweed.
7. Saccharin is not a sugar and so is not a food. It is an artificially prepared chemical that passes through the body undigested.
8. Mineral oils are not fats and so have no food value. They cannot be saponified and so also pass through the body undigested.
9. Hydrolysed protein on food labels means that some action has taken place, and the protein has been partially broken down.
10. Anabolic steroids are growth hormones that develop muscle.

11. Sorbitol and mannitol, which are sometimes used to sweeten diabetic foods, should be regarded as sugar as far as calories are concerned.

12. Glycogen is not eaten when we eat meat because it is quickly converted to glucose when the animal dies.

13. Some beans, such as soya beans and red kidney beans, contain proteins that can be harmful unless well-cooked.

14. Amino acids are only slightly affected by normal cooking, although all the tryptophan (an amino acid) is destroyed if meat is boiled for many hours.

15. Some oils that are massaged onto the skin are absorbed into the body and can be dangerous to pregnant women and epileptics.

16. High intakes of bran can reduce the absorption of essential minerals such as iron, calcium and zinc into the body.

17. Oily fish may reduce the chance of getting a heart attack. Oily fish include herring, salmon, sardines, sprats and mackerel.

18. Apricots and plum stones, as well as apple pips, contain cyanide.

19. Pickling foods increases their salt content.

20. Ingredients on food labels are listed in order of the amount that is put into the food. The largest amount first.

CHAPTER 11

WHY DOES THE BRAIN EAT THE BODY ON A CRASH DIET?

When someone goes on a crash diet, their brain will begin to eat their body. The brain depends on glucose as its main source of energy. The brain can survive for about five minutes without glucose. The brain then adapts to using ketones, which are produced by the breakdown of fat. Even when ketones provide fuel, the brain still needs glucose, and so it begins to use protein. The brain obtains this protein by breaking down muscle tissue.

Muscle tissue is made up mostly of protein, which is made up of amino acids. Normally, your body does not use protein to produce energy, but if your body runs out of glucose, it will begin to break down muscle tissue to release amino acids. These amino acids are converted in the liver to glucose in a process called gluconeogenesis.

If you try to lose weight too quickly, your brain will begin to eat your body, and the starvation response will be activated. You will then put all the weight you lose back on again. Be patient and lose weight slowly.

CHAPTER 12

THE STIMULI THE HYPOTHALAMUS NEEDS TO ACTIVATE THE STARVATION RESPONSE

It is easier to think of the hypothalamus as a room containing the clever little know-all. The four stimuli the clever, little know-all needs to activate the starvation response are:

1. A reduction in the number of calories consumed.
2. A reduction in the BMR.
3. A reduction in activity. (the MR)
4. The use of body fat to provide the body with fuel.

The two stimuli received by the clever little know-all when we go on the BC Diet are:

1. A reduction in the number of calories consumed.
2. The use of body fat to provide the body with fuel.

If someone exercises and their BMR and MR do not fall, but they go on a crash diet, their body will break down muscle to provide the brain with glucose. The brain will then begin to eat the body, and the starvation response will be activated.

If the clever little know-all receives the four stimuli, he will activate the starvation response, and all the weight you lose on a diet will be returned. On the BC Diet, the clever little know-all only receives two stimuli and the starvation response is not activated, and so the weight you lose will not be returned.

The clever little know-all controls many things in the human body, such as blood pressure, body temperature and body weight, by adhering to a set point, a process called Homeostasis.

When we go on a diet, the clever little know-all will be alerted. If he notices a reduction in the amount of food we are eating, a fall in our BMR, a reduction in our activity and that our body fat is being used as fuel, he will press the alarm button, and the starvation response will be activated. He needs all four stimuli before he presses the alarm button.

If we follow the BC Diet, the clever little know-all will see a reduction in the amount of food we are eating, and body fat being broken down and used as fuel. He will not see a reduction in our BMR, or a reduction in our activity, so he does not press the alarm button and the starvation response is not activated. Even though we are losing weight, he does not believe it is a famine. When we have lost weight, he will adjust our set point to our new weight, and we will stay slim.

In reality, there is no man inside our hypothalamus, and the hypothalamus does not think or reason. It only reacts to the stimuli it receives. If it does not receive the correct stimuli, it does not react.

The following example might help you to understand how the body reacts to stimuli. As well as a starvation response to a lack of food, we also possess a diving response that is activated by diving into water. These responses are survival mechanisms. To activate the diving response, we do not have to dive into water. All we need to do is insert our face into a bowl of water. Even though we are only inserting our face into a bowl of water, our brain thinks we are diving into water and reacts to the stimuli it receives by reducing blood flow to certain organs and lowering heart rate.

Altering the stimuli the hypothalamus receives is the only way to lose weight without activating the starvation response because we cannot alter our genes. We cannot take the starvation response out of our genes. This is why the BC Diet is the only way to lose weight and stay slim.

CHAPTER 13

HOW MUCH WEIGHT TO LOSE EACH WEEK

Activating the starvation response is a complicated process. It is better to be safe than sorry. If you lose too much weight, you could activate the starvation response. These are my recommendations for weight loss each week.

A small or inactive woman consuming 1,500 calories per day.

This person can safely lose an average of one pound per week without activating the starvation response.

A woman or a small man consuming 2,000 calories per day.

This person can safely lose an average of one and a half pounds per week without activating the starvation response.

A large woman or an inactive man consuming 2,500 calories per day.

This person can safely lose an average of two pounds per week without activating the starvation response.

An active man consuming 3,000 calories per day.

This person can safely lose an average of two and a half pounds per week without activating the starvation response.

A very active man consuming 3,500 calories per day.

This person can safely lose an average of three pounds per week without activating the starvation response.

CHAPTER 14

AN EXPLANATION OF MY CLAIM

My claim is that for most people, the Body-Controlled Diet is the only diet in the world that works if you want to lose weight and stay slim, that does not involve surgery or taking drugs.

I say for most people, because there is always the exception that proves the rule. I would expect The Body Controlled Diet to have a success rate of about 80%. The present success rate of people staying slim after dieting is between 3% and 5%. The reason I have said about 80% is because many people overeat because of mental and emotional problems. It is an unknown number, and could be even higher than 20%. No diet will work for them, I am afraid, until they sort out their problems.

As far as I know, there is no other way to lose weight other than by using the BC Diet method that does not activate the starvation response and the psychological cravings.

Printed in Dunstable, United Kingdom

77106865R00067